Your End
of Life Matters

Your End of Life Matters

How to Talk with Family and Friends

Anne Finkelman Ziff
LMFT, CGP, MA, MS

ROWMAN & LITTLEFIELD
Lanham · Boulder · New York · London

Published by Rowman & Littlefield
A wholly owned subsidiary of The Rowman & Littlefield Publishing Group, Inc.
4501 Forbes Boulevard, Suite 200, Lanham, Maryland 20706
www.rowman.com

Unit A, Whitacre Mews, 26-34 Stannary Street, London SE11 4AB

British Library Cataloguing in Publication Information Available

Library of Congress Cataloging-in-Publication Data
Names: Ziff, Anne F., author.
Title: Your end of life matters : How to Talk with family and friends / Anne Finkelman Ziff.
Description: Lanham : Rowman & Littlefield, [2018] | Includes bibliographical references and index.
Identifiers: LCCN 2017058541 (print) | LCCN 2018006457 (ebook) | ISBN 9781538110225 (electronic) | ISBN 9781538110218 (cloth : alk. paper)
Subjects: LCSH: Death—Handbooks, manuals, etc.
Classification: LCC GT3150 (ebook) | LCC GT3150 .Z47 2018 (print) | DDC 306.9—dc23
LC record available at https://lccn.loc.gov/2017058541

∞™ The paper used in this publication meets the minimum requirements of American National Standard for Information Sciences—Permanence of Paper for Printed Library Materials, ANSI/NISO Z39.48-1992.

Printed in the United States of America

I dedicate this book first, to my parents, Emanuel David and Helen Cohen Finkelman, without whose generosity, wisdom, and love it would not exist. Their memory is indeed for a blessing.

Second, I dedicate this book with great appreciation to each person who shared with me the stories that have been incorporated into this volume. I hope that in return, they received a full measure of conversation and satisfaction.

Third, I dedicate the book to my daughters, Debby and Amy; my sons-in-law, Jamie and Jeff; and my four beloved grandchildren, Kostya, Ali, Zach, and Ani. I hope that conversations and love continue always to be a vital part of our relationships.

Contents

Foreword

Walton H. Ehrhardt

*Y**our End of Life Matters: How to Talk with Family and Friends* is a book for *everyone*, from adolescents to those of us who are considerably older! It is also a book for professional "helpers" of every variety. I say this wearing at least two hats, first as an ordained clergy in the Lutheran Church in America (ELCA), and former pastor to three churches when I became consultant to the Bishop of the TX/LA Gulf Coast Synod of the ELCA until 2016. In my second hat, I am licensed in Louisiana as Marriage and Family Therapist and Supervisor; a faculty member of the International Psychotherapy Institute, Chevy Chase, Maryland; and maintain a private psychotherapy practice in Greater New Orleans. I tell you this to emphasize the nature of my experience as well as my enthusiasm for the tone and information Anne Ziff offers in this timely new book, in which she quickly captures the reader's attention, speaking plainly from a position that has become somewhat "uncommon" today. . . . Anne is *real*. She has written from the experiences of having been there, and the reader is drawn in by her personal story, her conviction,

I first met Anne Ziff almost thirty years ago while training at the Washington School of Psychiatry in its two-year Object Relations Theory and Therapy Program. In the many large- and small-group experiences, I rapidly became aware of her capabilities and her demonstrated leadership in our field of individual, couple, family, and group therapy; she was a creative-spirited woman, very intelligent, and quite the innovator. Anne was real and caring; pretense was not her hallmark. From that beginning emerged an endearing and enduring friendship that expanded to include my wife, both of us blessed by Anne's warmth and generosity. So I must admit that I am deeply honored by her request to convey my evaluation of this work. I am delighted that Anne has produced another contribution intended to help us all with "issues connected to our humanity" (as I think of the vicissitudes of life). I am excited that *Your End of Life Matters* has arrived; a book like this is long overdue and certainly welcome at this point in time!

Your End of Life Matters is a compilation of fascinating, intensely personal stories and writing exercises, woven into a "how-to" communication book, focusing on the topic of end-of-life matters—your own! It is not a guide to assist you in writing your Last Will and Testament (although the author does advocate creating one if you have not already done so.) Nor does the book offer directions in making a Living Will, although Legacy Documents are considered.

Each chapter addresses a significant aspect in the otherwise daunting task of becoming aware of the issues, and then, talking with at least one significant other about your end-of-life matters.

Face-to-face conversation has declined sharply in the past 20 years. Anne encourages personal communication and guides readers to make these be successful. She is zealous in stressing the point that the person we choose to *listen* to us must be willing and able to hear and respect our wishes and desires. We need to be wary of settling for someone who will give lip service to assent, while having no intention to follow through on your wishes. The examples of such behaviors that she cites are chilling, if not downright infuriating.

A heads-up call to human relationship professionals, this book is for us, too! We who are attorneys, clergy, counselors, couple and family therapists, physicians, psychologists, social workers, teachers, and more—we human relationship specialists are facing a population that is increasingly losing connection with the essence and core of its being. I have devoted fifty-plus years to working in close, frequently intense, emotional, highly personal relationships with people who struggle with serious life-matters. I will categorically state: **This guide is a *gift* that I regret not having possessed in the past to recommend to individual people in need**, or as Anne suggests, to utilize also with groups of people, teaching some to lead others in working through these important matters. I once again emphasize, and this is one of the most significant aspects about this book: *it is for everyone*—for all human beings.

As a professional psychotherapist, I conclude sadly that too many of us do not give enough attention and time to experience one another on emotionally intimate levels. We succumb to pretense. When we are not being real with our emotions, we are easily led into addictions, especially those teased by technology and our electronic gadgets. Anne challenges readers to face their *emotions* and share them. What matters to you? That question forms the backdrop of this book. More specifically, *what are the important elements that you deem significant about living your life as you consider ultimately mov-*

*ing toward its end? What matters especially **before** you will be experiencing that "finality"?* Clearly, *Your End of Life Matters: How to Talk with Family and Friends* is a different kind of book.

Permit me to make a point with a personal anecdote. In October 2014, my wife and I were introduced to Vice President Job Biden by our youngest son, a Secret Service agent assigned to Biden's detail, on the tarmac of New Orleans International Airport. We had no idea of the intimacy of their relationship. I was prepared to hear some political rhetoric or pitch coming from the Vice President. But, No! What I experienced was a stranger who introduced himself to us as "Joe Biden" and connected with us by *risking* the *opening* of his heart and soul, *baring* his own pain in identification with the horror of unbearable grief from losing someone beloved—in his case, most recently, his son to cancer and in ours, our young daughter to accidental drowning many years before. The three of us shared personal testimony of loss. *What is so significant for this book discussion is the willingness to be a Listener, to hear and to receive with respect.* In that moment on the tarmac, our hearts could echo the intimacy of significant sharing among three vulnerable human beings talking about that which truly matters. Let yours do this, too.

Back to the book! All of us can and do procrastinate. Many readers anticipate great difficulty in speaking about the end of their own lives and so they put it off. Trouble is, they're not the ones who'll suffer from this denial. It's their family and friends, who'll be left with the burden of wondering if they're doing "the right thing." Reluctant though you may be, have this conversation. Do it, follow Anne's lead, and then go on *living* your life, as she recommends.

I am convinced you will join me in gratitude by reading and using to its fullest *Your End of Life Matters: How to Talk with Family and Friends,* for yourself and for those you care about most.

—**Walton H. Ehrhardt**, EdD
Mandeville, Louisiana

Introduction

Genius is the ability to put into effect what is on your mind.

—F. Scott Fitzgerald, American Author (1896–1940)

I promise you, neither I nor anyone else thinks of me as possessing "genius." I do, however, very much want to put into effect something that is on my mind and that I believe is relevant to everyone: personal experience has taught me how important and valuable it is to think about, and then talk with someone trustable about, your end-of-life matters.

I do believe that going through this process can be beneficial for virtually everyone, but the best I can do is reach out to you, one reader at a time, and let word of mouth do the rest. How do I do that? I encourage you to read this book, and let yourself be moved.

The radically changing climate about end-of-life medical options and care in our culture is bringing these issues to the forefront of a larger conversation. In fact, in 2016, Medicare began to allow physicians to receive payment for time spent discussing these specific topics with their patients. Be a participant in this if you have the time and inclination. *Your End of Life Matters* offers you the chance to take advantage of the recent changes in our society, and to learn some things about yourself that may please and surprise you.

I wonder . . . What's made you curious enough or enticed you to begin reading this book? Was it the full title: *Your End of Life Matters: How to Talk with Family and Friends*? Is this conversation one you've been thinking about on your own? Did you welcome the opportunity to learn how to talk effectively about your end-of-life thoughts? Has some special event triggered your interest—a milestone birthday, anniversary, or graduation, perhaps? Has a friend just received a troubling diagnosis? Have you lost someone dear to

A Place for Thoughts

At various times throughout this book, I'm going to suggest that you make some notes. It'll be a good idea for you to decide now how you'd like to do this and prepare accordingly to have handy everything you're going to need.

- You may want to use a pen or pencils of any kind or color.
- You may choose to write on a pad of paper.
- You may prefer to find a special notebook that you'd like to use as a journal to accompany your reading of *Your End of Life Matters*.
- You may prefer to do your writing with any kind of electronic device—cell phone, iPad, laptop, or full-size desktop computer.

Choose whatever method you prefer for responding to the writing prompts and exercises throughout the chapters. Be sure you choose a method that will meet the following criteria:

- Ensure your privacy.
- Be readily accessible when it is time for you to carry out the writing prompts and exercises (or to look back later at a prompt from another chapter).
- Be available in the moments you feel inspired to do some personal writing of your own spontaneous thoughts.
- Be available for notes, poetry, vignettes, and so on, that catch your attention at any time while you're working with the material in the chapters that follow.

you or been particularly touched attending a funeral? You may simply be at a stage in life where you are taking little for granted, and you no longer are denying your own mortality. Expressing your wishes may be helpful to you as you move away from denial and into some of the vulnerable experiences of being mortal that help you appreciate and live your life more fully.

These are just *some* of the many and varied reasons you might approach thinking about the end of your life, whether that seems imminent—or not. Whether your need is immediate or more "down the road," this book provides support and guidance to you as you consider how to talk about end-of-life matters, either your own or those of someone you care about. Read on to learn more.

WHY NOW?

As you will read in detail in chapter 1, the impetus for me to write this book was a taboo-breaking telephone call from my parents when I was in my thirties. Throughout the book, I tell you my stories and pieces of stories I have heard, either in general conversation or as I worked as a marriage and family therapist, group leader, and so on. These stories are culled variously from conversations with workshop participants, patients, friends, colleagues, and physicians of disciplines other than psychiatry, nearly all of whom have encouraged me to create this book for them and for you now, rather than later. In general, however, I have made changes in the stories as needed in order to preserve the privacy of the people involved.

HOW CAN YOU MAKE GOOD USE OF THIS BOOK?

Strange as this may seem, I suggest that you take a moment right now, before you read further in this introduction, to give careful consideration to my question of what led you to read this book. Consider how you'd like to respond and, without spending more than three to five minutes on this exercise, jot down your thoughts in a journal you can choose right now—perhaps a handy electronic device, or a paper notepad or notebook, or something else you'd prefer. (It's likely that you'll want to return to these responses as you read something in later chapters that tweaks your memory. You may want to revise your choice of actual journal, as well.)

WHY ARE THESE
END-OF-LIFE CONVERSATIONS VALUABLE?

The intrinsic value of an actual end-of-life conversation is important without question, but it's not the whole story. There's a figurative rainbow out there, waiting to reveal itself when the work required for having a satisfying end-of-life conversation has been successfully completed, and you're clearly still alive and ready to move on with living.

A rainbow? Yes. Ultimately these conversations make life easier to live—both for the person who initiates the talking and for the Listener(s) to those thoughts and wishes! It reminds me of finding the pot of gold at the end of a rainbow—a little something extra for your trouble.

HOW TO USE THIS BOOK

Option 1: Be an Independent Reader

Your End of Life Matters is easy to read on your own. It emphasizes the importance of perspective, good humor, and clarity when discussing considerations for the end of your own life. Once you have thought about, spoken about, and dealt with this material as comfortably as possible for you, you will likely discover that a significant amount of anxiety about the prospect of the end of your life fades away. This is such a highly desirable outcome, of course, that you may look for someone else to talk to about your (enlightening) experience. There's nothing wrong with that. What's more, the person you choose to share the experience with is likely to welcome your information. It's a little bit like going to a movie that you hadn't expected to like very much but coming out captured by it. When you rush to tell your friends, they are likely to want to go to that very movie and see if it affects them the same way. So, too, the life experience of a satisfying conversation.

I encourage you to read *Your End of Life Matters* and let it function quite purposely as a catalyst to living more fully. Some of the stories and various exercises included in the book make it possible for you to think about topics related to your own end-of-life matters, any number of which you may previously have considered unthinkable and even unmentionable.

In the context of *Your End of Life Matters*, you can now consider and discuss these issues with the people who will be most interested and involved. I hope you will indeed experience the relief that can come from being able to identify, demystify, face, and talk about your end-of-life needs and wishes.

Option 2: Consider a Book Group

When I facilitate groups or workshops about end-of-life communication, I keep the groups small so we have adequate time for working with the writing prompts and exercises and for talking at each meeting. We usually meet in groups of six to ten people, sitting either in a circle or around a table. You may be interested in doing something similar by reading this book as part of a long-term book group. In that forum, you'll have opportunities for conversation, to swap stories, to discuss entries in your journal if you choose to, and to get some help when you're puzzled or stuck about what to do next. Appendix A has a guide for book groups, which I hope you'll make use of whether you're the group leader or simply one of the actively participating members.

(Even if you are just reading on your own, you may find some of the group suggestions useful.)

Please note that when two or three friends read the same book and discuss it informally, that also qualifies as a book group. Who, if anyone, you read this book with and the specifics of how you do that are entirely up to you. You are welcome to make use of the guide or not, under any circumstances.

WHAT TO DO AFTER YOUR CONVERSATION

Once your end-of-life conversation is accomplished, it is time for you to get on with your life and live it as fully as you know how. That's an important realization, and I'll mention it to you from time to time throughout this book.

Sharon was a participant in one of my groups. She looked young, vital, and healthy at seventy-two. She was quiet during the initial "get to know me" go-round. Toward the end, she spoke out.

"Old age is life's greatest surprise. It's much trickier than living with someone you thought you knew well and loved!" she joked. "There's no knowing in advance when it will hit, if, or how. But in my case, it hit me without warning two years after I retired," she went on. "Suddenly I'm diagnosed as having a debilitating neurological illness, and frankly, I'm terrified." There was a long pause before she concluded, "This is the first time I've said the words out loud; even my husband doesn't know."

The group was quiet and seemed shocked after Sharon spoke. One or two thanked her for trusting us, and an older man said that if he were her husband, he'd want her to take a chance and trust him to know both what was wrong and what she wanted from him. Sharon got teary eyed and nodded.

She continued to attend the group sessions, did the exercises, and wrote privately, sharing very little in the group. However, nearly two months later, at our last session, when each participant shared "mission—or conversation—accomplished," Sharon smiled shyly and asked to speak first.

"Deep breath!" she whispered to herself.

"I've done it! I've talked to my husband, told him everything we learned to prepare here, and he's agreed to all I prefer. I know he'll be there for me in the ways that matter to me. And also, I feel so much better since we talked the way we learned to do here, that, at least for the time being, I've stopped seeing my therapist for anxiety!" She grinned. And the group applauded.

The acknowledgment that death will ultimately happen to each of us amplifies the importance of fully living your own life, whatever its length and other dimensions. I hope you, too, will grow to appreciate, value, and put into action the information that *Your End of Life Matters* offers you. Doing so will help you free yourself from many of the worries or fears that too easily become compounded by silence.

The completion of this project typically offers you the experience of having a burden lifted, enjoying a new ease and capacity for making choices and decisions, and following that rainbow to check out the pot of gold for yourself.

I invite you to read on. Chapter 1 has a real-life, taboo-breaking story to tell you.

—Anne Finkelman Ziff
New York, New York
September 2017

1

Free Yourself from Worries and Fears; Read a Story

Life shrinks or expands in proportion to one's courage.

—Anaïs Nin, American Author (1903–1977)

SETTING THE STAGE

*L*ike the majority of parents, mine were far from perfect, but they did a lot of things I realize in retrospect were really valuable, and I've attempted to emulate with my own family. One is particularly relevant to this book. Suspend your disbelief, please, and read my story.

I was in my thirties, the divorced, single mother of eight- and ten-year-old daughters, living in Westport, Connecticut, home to writers, actors, and many New York City commuters of various occupations. I fit in the *writer* and *commuter* categories. Evenings were always busy, and it was rare that my parents would call us during the week. When my telephone rang this particular night, shortly after our dinner, the girls had already left the kitchen to do homework; I was finishing cleaning up, changing a load of laundry, and beginning to think about tomorrow's lunches.

BREAKING A TABOO—A LONG STORY

"Do you have a few minutes? Daddy and I want to talk with you," began this unexpected weeknight call from my mother.

"Of course, we can talk! Let me just tell the girls not to disturb us," I replied. This was odd enough that I immediately directed my two young daughters not to interrupt us unless there was an emergency.

"So, what's up?" I asked, returning to the telephone. (These were still the days when stationary landlines were all we had for telephones.)

"Daddy's on the extension," my mother noted, and then continued.

"We just had an interesting dinner with Faye and Al." (These were friends of my parents who lived in their Brooklyn, New York, apartment building.)

"And you're calling to tell me that?" I asked, incredulous.

"Oh, no. We just wanted to give you some context. We expect that they're talking to their sons just like we're calling you, in fact."

"Um, what about?" I asked, listening carefully and still feeling pretty anxious.

"Well, honey," my mother began, "we just want to have this conversation with you. And we want to ask you a few questions, too."

At this point, I was totally in the dark and very confused. My anxiety was growing. This didn't feel like a benign start to an ordinary, casual conversation. What, exactly, was on their minds? I had no idea. There was an extended silence while I waited for one of them to proceed.

My mother spoke up. "When we die, Anne, are you going to want to have a funeral for us, or a memorial service, or what?"

"What? What are you trying to tell me?" I remember exclaiming. "Who's sick? What's going on here? Why are we talking about funerals or memorial services? What aren't you telling me?"

Obviously, I was caught by surprise, unnerved, and hugely worried by the question I had just heard my mother pose.

"Seriously," I offered, in an attempt to collect myself and not derail their intended remarks. "Why are you asking me this?"

"Honey, we just want to talk with you about what you'll need. We really want you to think about it. No one's sick, but we'd like to talk with you about what you'll want, when the time comes for each of us."

"Well, really, I haven't the faintest idea! I've never thought about it at all. **What do you want?**" I countered.

"It's not something we think we should decide, Anne. It'll be for you at that point; we'll be gone," my mother said calmly. "I think you can just close your eyes and picture what'll feel best for you after one of us has passed away. Just try it, like meditating or when you do guided imagery."

At first I thought that I would have to tell them I needed more time to think, but I closed my eyes the way you'd start for a guided meditation, breathing deeply and slowly, and attempted to imagine that one of my parents had died. What would I want? (Right then I was wishing my parents would have had something in mind to tell me to do, but clearly, that wasn't what they thought was appropriate or necessary.)

The meditating attempt took me some time. Eventually, my resistance ebbed away, and I began to have a sense that I'd want people around me and to be involved in some familiar type of ritual. I pictured very little visually, but felt a great sense of loss and of wanting support from other people. That translated in my mind to a funeral and also to the Jewish tradition of sitting shiva that follows.

"Okay, I think I'll want a funeral for you."

"That's fine, then," responded my mother. She proceeded to give me details about who should conduct the service, where it should be held, and at what time of day.

"What?" I blurted, surprised at the way they had these details at their fingertips. "What's going on that you've got this all planned out? Why are we talking about this all of a sudden? Who is sick?"

"Anne," my father said, speaking up on his own for the first time, "Al just brought up their idea of having this conversation tonight at dinner. He and Faye have been planning it out for about a month now, and wanted to give it a dry run with us. Your mother and I thought the conversation was such a good idea that we decided to call you when we got home and talk with you just like they're doing with their boys. Mother and I feel we know everything that you need to know, and we're prepared to give you a lot of information tonight. That's all!"

"That's all?" was what was in my mind. They were, at the very least, knocking my socks off! And they thought I'd believe this was "just" to give me some information? A casual conversation? Ha.

"You're really not sick, either one of you?" I demanded, still anxious.

"We're fine," they said in chorus.

"I hope so!" I responded. "Although I have to say you've taken me by surprise with this. I kind of wish you'd given me some kind of advance notice."

"I guess if we'd been planning it for a while, we might have thought to do that." My mother was listening closely as we spoke, and she agreed, explaining, "But it just came to mind when Faye and Al brought it up at dinner, so we came home, pulled out a bunch of papers with addresses and account numbers and so on, and we called you. Really very simple!"

My father took over the call. It became significantly more businesslike. I quickly got a pad of paper from my desk and prepared to write as the rest of our conversation developed. (It would have been easier with a computer, of course, but this was before computers as well as cell phones.) What followed was a detailed list relating to burial decisions, bank accounts, safe deposit boxes, and physicians' and attorneys' names, office addresses, telephone numbers, and so on. Data for friends and their rabbi was also included.

My father admonished me to be sure to save this personal information in a place that would be safe, even if I moved. I filed my notes both in my memory, where they were indelibly etched at once, and in a labeled folder in the file cabinet at my desk. An only child, I had suddenly become the permanent, solo Listener to all of their end-of-life wishes and pertinent data.

Fast forward to June 1986, eight years after this unconventional, taboo-breaking telephone call my parents had initiated. While their information was indeed etched in my brain as well as documented on paper, it had rarely surfaced in my thoughts during the intervening years as we carried on with our lives in ordinary ways. For a couple in their seventies in the 1970s, my parents were active and healthy. Over time, I had grown to trust that their motive for initiating that taboo-breaking conversation with me truly had been advance planning, not some concealed, urgent need.

Thus, we expected no complications when my mother underwent hip replacement surgery. The procedure went well. I was allowed to visit her in the intensive care unit, and she was resting comfortably as I left in the early evening. So when the surgeon called around 11:00 p.m. to tell me my mother had died suddenly of a heart attack, it threw me totally. First I cried, and then I felt panic, as grief set in and the parade of "what do we do now" questions marched in front of me.

Suddenly, out of what seemed like nowhere, I experienced a very welcome sense of calm and clarity. Through the chaos, I thought back to that disconcerting telephone call from nearly ten years earlier, and as I did, I realized that I had no need for my filed notes. Everything my mother and father had told me was now vivid in my memory and provided, readily, the answers to virtually all the questions I was suddenly having to address.

Although that conversation had begun without fanfare, reflecting back on it, it was one of the most useful, influential, and loving gifts imaginable. I was only just beginning to recognize its value that chaotic evening and in the days that followed my mother's unexpected death. But eventually, that recognition led me to think and talk about how lucky I was that we had actually discussed all these details about end-of-life matters, and why everyone should consider doing the same thing. This book is a compendium of my thoughts and my experiences in talking about end-of-life matters with a broad base of colleagues and people in my therapy practice, as well as with friends and family. Join us!

NOW IT'S YOUR TURN

What Do You Specifically Hope to Gain from This Book?

What is it that enticed you to be reading this book? Was it the promise of learning how to have a conversation about *your own* end-of-life thoughts and desires? Perhaps you have family members whom you'd like to help do this for *themselves?*

You may simply believe in planning ahead, and having already discussed and created your estate plan or Last Will and Testament with an attorney or financial planner, you are at a loss as to how to ensure that someone will see that your wishes are carried out or when to arrange for that. Whatever your reason, it's likely that you hope this book will help you (or someone you care about) safely and effectively express end-of-life wishes. I hope so, too.

Your End of Life Matters tells stories in every chapter—my stories and those of colleagues, friends, or people I have worked with who took the chance to break the taboo, to crack open the silence around end-of-life matters. It also offers "how to" exercises and writing prompts that are intended to help you move through the text and process your own thoughts. Whether your need is immediate or simply down the road a bit, this book provides support and guidance to you while you think about if, why, how—and when—to communicate end-of-life matters, either your own or those of someone you care about. *In carrying out your plan to talk about end-of-life concerns, I think you will discover, as I have ultimately, that there's a surprising new freedom in the*

A Starting Point

Strange as this may seem, I want you to start right now with a writing prompt, to create a piece of your own story. Take a moment, before you read further, to consider the initial question below and jot down your reason(s) for reading *Your End of Life Matters*. You'll probably want to refer to your notes as you read further in the book; it's convenient to keep them handy.

In your journal, start on an empty page with the following heading: **What I specifically hope to gain from reading this book.** List all the reasons that occur to you now, and leave space on the page for others that may occur as you get further into the book.

*ways we live and think about doing the right things—throughout life, starting at any age at all when talking about end-of-life matters feels right. Perhaps **you** are ready to check this out now.*

THE GIFT OF A LIFETIME AND HOW I HAVE CHOSEN TO USE IT

Although I had no way to recognize it as such at the time, that long-ago telephone conversation was *the gift of a lifetime* and possibly the most generous, helpful gift my parents ever gave me. Nearly four decades later, I find myself still recognizing and remarking upon how ultimately valuable to me that simple, direct conversation was. I certainly had no way of predicting how much relief I would feel, knowing that I was doing exactly what my mother had told me she wanted when she and my father initiated that telephone conversation. But I knew it very soon after her death, and then my father's, and I know it now without a doubt and share it widely.

This very personal episode was the first seed planted for this book. Subsequent stories from people I've worked with, colleagues, relatives, and friends further nourished that seed, and as I've lectured, the requests for an actual book were ultimately persuasive. A combination of experience and needs convinced me to write the book you are now reading. Its foundation, based on my family's story, is amplified with stories from other families and combined with text, humor, and writing prompts (exercises) in the chapters that follow to help you consider the value to *you, now,* of a conversation about end-of-life matters for yourself and also for your family. Chapter 2 illustrates the value of stories as we move through this material.

2

Learn from Stories

Any problem, big or small, within a family, always seems to start with bad communication. Someone isn't listening.

—Emma Thompson, English Actress (1959–)

STORIES HELP US LISTEN AND LEARN

*F*or centuries, stories have been used to capture attention, teach values, illustrate and dramatize principles, and help people live their lives. Drama, initially from the portals of the church, brought to life stories that are still vital today. In this tradition, I use stories from my own life and from friends, workshop participants, colleagues, and clinical therapy clients to form the central teaching tool of this book. No matter what your circumstances, I anticipate that something in one or more of the stories will strike a chord, reveal a solution, or inspire action having to do with your own end-of-life matters. *Although we often seek "answers" to our questions, what's most pertinent is apt to be stories—from which we're back to figuring out the answers for ourselves!* Some people are lucky enough to recognize how valuable stories are even before they get old. Are you one of them?

In my childhood, I had learned that talking was important and not to be avoided, even when it wasn't easy. When a two-year-old I know had just become big sister she wasn't happy and had her own way of coping. One day, she climbed on my lap, saying only, "I'm gonna tell you a story." When her litany of disappointments was finished, her story ended. She kissed my cheek, climbed down, left me with all her discharged feelings, and scampered off, happy. Talking IS important—at any age!

Listening is an equally important, required aspect of successful conversations. As a therapist, I recognize that the gift of talking together, engaging comfortably in conversation, is not everyone's childhood experience. Whether or not your experiences with stories began in childhood, as an adult, it is entirely possible to expand the repertoire of your family and friendships to include conversation, with *listening and remembering* being as important a demonstrated skill as *speaking*.

I believe that it's never too late to begin to talk together, to bring out in the open the thoughts that are on your mind, to communicate. To a large extent, the stories, text, and writing prompts throughout *Your End of Life Matters* are intended specifically to add to your ability to process your end-of-life matters (the data and wishes) and to increase your comfort talking about them—with or without much previous experience in having comparable discussions. *There's no right or wrong, only personal feelings, to guide you through this process of talking about what you hope for or picture best for yourself at the end of your life.* Initiators (see below) will want to convey information and feelings. Listeners will want to listen without judgments, accept the information, and ask questions when clarification is needed. When it is their turn to talk as well, Listeners must speak honestly—about their willingness or reluctance to proceed, or anything else they are thinking about on this topic.

PARTNERS IN CONVERSATION

It's readily understood that a conversation implies the involvement of more than one participant. At least two people are present in all conversations. These delicate, end-of-life discussions are no exception. As you are recognizing, throughout this book, I divide conversation participants into two types: Initiators and Listeners. Sometimes a Listener will grow to also be an Initiator, as in my case. At other times, someone who starts out as a probable Listener becomes instead an Initiator—as was the case for Jimmy, whose story I describe in chapter 4.

In the context of this book, an *Initiator* is a person of any age or gender who believes that it is appropriate to *initiate,* or start, a conversation. For our purposes, that conversation pertains to end-of-life considerations, wishes, documents, and other data. The conversation will be directed to or with the person I refer to as the *Listener,* or the one who receives the information set forth by the conversation's Initiator. The Listener, like the Initiator, can be a person of any age or gender. When an Initiator prefers, there can be more than one Listener.

The Listener is the person who listens to and receives the end-of-life wishes of another person, as well as any relevant information about documents, finances, and so on, and who *agrees to carry out these wishes* when the time comes. While having this conversation is primarily to the Initiator's advantage, Listeners will derive many benefits from it as well, as my story and those of other Listeners described throughout this book demonstrate.

The terms *Initiator* and *Listener* may seem artificial or awkward initially, but they are easy enough to understand and use. I began this book with my story, in which I was the Listener of an unexpected but totally valuable telephone conversation with my parents, who were the Initiators. This conversation has become part of our family lore and history, as well as our collective memory. I recognized that the day would come when it would be my turn to initiate.

To my surprise, when I acted on my own need to initiate a conversation with my adult daughters as the Listeners, I was taken aback, disappointed even, that none of this foreknowledge made it easier for me or them to willingly and actively move forward. It was harder than I'd hoped or expected for me to be the Initiator and, as a result, I was slow getting started, and a bit reluctant to talk about it.

I've worked with some families who report also that, as Listeners, their adult children seem to be absolutely resistant to planning a time to get together and talk. I understand and appreciate adult children's reluctance to accede to making this a priority. I might very well have procrastinated if I'd had the opportunity to put off my parents' conversation! Initiators, however, are human, are apt to feel vulnerable, and can easily be frustrated instead of flattered by the denial of their mortality that Listener reluctance to commit to a conversation can convey.

While I separate the Initiator/Listener roles for purposes of discussion, some of you may find yourself playing both roles for a time—yourself initiating a discussion with a parent showing early signs of dementia, for example, in order to eventually become the Listener of the same parent's information. Such is the case for Karen and her brother, Arnold. They both live on the East Coast, and their parents are in Seattle, Washington. Their mom has begun to repeat herself in such a way that they have each become concerned. Dad, however, stays entrenched in denial. The "kids" want to bring their parents east for a visit, during which they'd like to *initiate* their parents' conversation. In order to rebut the sudden parental reluctance to travel, Karen has decided to fly to Seattle on a business trip and then fly east with her folks to facilitate their travel and visit. Arnold arranged to fly back with them at the end of their two-week visit, ostensibly for a "business" purpose of his own. It may take more than one visit to complete the conversation to everyone's satisfaction, a not uncommon situation that I'll address later in the book.

RECOGNIZE THAT THIS
PARTNERSHIP HAS MANY OPTIONS

Sometimes the Initiator/Listener roles are not based on typical or anticipated age-related roles. In one complicated family situation, after both parents had died, a mature woman I worked with initiated a conversation with her elder brother, whose behavior had become inconsistent and irrational. She feared that he, in his current role as titular head of their family, could not manage the responsibilities of their complicated estates. She initiated a conversation with him, stating clearly what her own wants and needs were, and asked if he felt able to carry this through for her when the time came. He listened and gave thought to her request and admitted that he didn't think he could comply. In this case, the Initiator had to continue her search for a trustworthy Listener not only for her own matters but also for those of other family members. To further complicate her task, this brother took to heart her own described needs and reversed the roles, asking her to listen to and carry out his own end-of-life wishes. Relieved to be able to clear up the ambiguities in their estate in the future, she agreed. Then she moved forward to initiate her own end-of-life-matters conversation a second time, with a new Listener, one who was more affirming of her requests. Although the response was a "no," in this case, careful listening brought the family to a clear communication with a good outcome.

In another instance, my clients were Sue and Jeff, a retired couple in their late sixties. They had seen some friends die suddenly and watched as another friend was diminished by dementia. As a couple, they strove to be realistic. They were united in wanting to enjoy these "senior" years for as long as they were together in good health and had financial security from one source or another. They became excited to plan new adventures, rather than feeling sad because of losses or changes.

Sue and Jeff worked together with me in my office and made multiple notes about the conversation they wanted to initiate. In much the same way, you will use this book and your own notes to develop the conversation *you* want to initiate. In due time, Sue and Jeff took the necessary deep breath and invited their children, who would be their conversation's Listeners, to visit them for "brunch and conversation" one weekend. "We can initiate this conversation in style!" was the couple's mantra. And they did.

Admittedly, Sue and Jeff had a lot going for them: love, good health, financial security, and a sense of adventure and good humor as well. Not everyone has all of that. But *what I believe each person does have is the ability to individually decide who you are, what matters to you now, who should know this information, and how to make that happen.*

This is something you *can* do, whether you are married or part of a life partnership, have been single for your whole life, or became single more recently in one manner or another. It's true whether or not you are a parent. Let's face it, not all parents have children who live conveniently nearby, nor have all parents been able to develop healthy, loving relationships with each child. Yet even curmudgeonly parents are able to be the Initiator of a conversation, and sometimes the Listener they find actually will be one of their children.

LET EXERCISES GUIDE YOUR CONVERSATION PREPARATIONS

Behavioral scientists recognize the value of setting tangible goals to provide a focus for action and change. In a similar way, the writing prompts and exercises I present throughout this book can help you focus on, and provide an increased sense of ease about, initiating an end-of-life conversation that fits your style and needs. Your thoughts and choices are exclusively up to you. I have no intention of telling you what to think or how to feel about the end of your life. The stories and exercises in this book may provide clues and suggestions for you, to help you ferret out some uniquely personal information that is likely to guide your talk about what is important to you.

There are some general suggestions to keep in mind as you work with the proposed exercises throughout the book. Let me remind you here of what they are:

1. Set up a journal so that all your responses are in one single resource. Keep it simple, accessible, and convenient—whether paper and pencil, electronic file, or even audio/videotape. Use whatever form is most comfortable for you.
2. Make use of your responses in a way that works for you—to simply sort through pertinent questions and thoughts, to learn some things about yourself that you hadn't been aware of, or even to begin to develop a script for your actual conversation.
3. Be honest. No one else need ever see your responses.

4. "Now" may not feel like the time to do any given exercise. That's not a problem. In your journal, simply make a note to return here later on when the time is right. Perhaps something in another chapter will stimulate your responses or change your mind. Any time that feels right to you is the right time to proceed with any exercise you find in this book, including the ones that follow here.

EXERCISE: PUT YOURSELF IN MY SHOES

Earlier in this book, I told you a rather detailed story of my own experience as a Listener, with my parents as the Initiators. What I suggest now is that you take a few minutes and "put yourself in my shoes." I'll guide you to learn a bit about your own capacity for empathy (the process of identifying with the thoughts, feelings, or actions of someone else) and for distancing (the process of moving away from a person, story, or feeling because of your sense of discomfort or anxiety). Take a moment to review my family's story in chapter 1, if you need to, and then allow yourself to consider the following questions:

1. As you think about the conversation my parents initiated, with whom do you identify, the Initiators or the Listener? What factors lead you to feel that way?
2. If you were to talk like this to someone you care about, how do you picture yourself—as Initiator or Listener? Why do you think this?
3. If you were the Listener of a conversation presented in a manner similar to this one, what do you think your response might have been?
4. If you were the Initiator of a conversation like the one I described, how do you think you'd be feeling when it ended?

When you have finished working with this exercise, you are apt to recognize in yourself a predisposition either to feel empathy or the desire to distance. Either or both of these characteristics will be useful to observe as you do your own work with end-of-life conversations, and, in fact, with conversations and relationships in general.

EXERCISE: MAKE YOURSELF COMFORTABLE

People are typically uncomfortable talking openly about topics that they consider taboo. In our culture, sex has commonly been one such topic. Aging is another. Taking a chapter from sex therapy, I help people develop comfort with, and "desensitize" to, both the concepts and the words *aging* and *end of life* by looking the descriptive, perhaps unflattering or frightening, terms straight on. The desired result is that the negative power of the offending words or terms is diminished, and they may even become laughable. Remember the childhood taunt "Sticks and stones may break my bones, but words can never harm me"? That's true in this adult case as well. At least I anticipate that it will be, after you've done the following desensitization exercise.

1. Limit yourself to five minutes to make a list of any and all the words and expressions you can think of that have to do with getting older, aging, and illness. Here are a few common examples: bucket list, CRS (slang: can't remember shit), death, dementia, senility.
2. If you need further inspiration, see appendix B.
3. Read your list aloud (to yourself—no audience needed).
4. Which of these words do you AVOID using in general?
5. Which of these words are you typically able to use?
6. Write **one sentence**, using any of the aging-related words you are comfortable with, to describe yourself. (One example: "I'm nowhere near *senility*, but sometimes I indeed have *CRS*, and I have now begun a *bucket list* for myself after years of making fun of people who keep one.")
7. And now a challenge: Write one more sentence, using at least two of the words you really usually shy away from!

Regardless of how you welcome or deny the aging process, having completed this exercise, you are likely to have developed a greater sense of comfort in being a participant in talking about aging. As Lady Bird Johnson and others have said, "*Growing old isn't so bad when you consider the alternative.*" In the next chapter, we'll look at one way to structure your preparations for this end-of-life conversation that will ensure your personal definition of its success.

3

Lay the Groundwork

One has to grow up with good talk in order to form the habit of it.

—Helen Hayes, American Actress (1900–1993)

*Y*our end-of-life conversation is one I hope you'll be satisfied with, one you will feel confident about before and after it takes place. This decision will be yours, but I hope you will ultimately choose to have an end-of-life conversation of your own. Its planning and execution are important, and very personal. Since that's the case, we'll spend time in this chapter exploring elements of successful conversations, what they feel like, and how you can increase your chances of having one that will please *you*, particularly on this sensitive topic, end-of-life matters. We'll also look at the varieties of families that exist and how differences among them might affect the way you think, or talk successfully, about your end-of-life wishes.

Conversations are an essential ingredient of virtually all successful forms of communication in relationships. For some of us, the habit of good talking began in childhood; we grew up with it. For others, the habit of "good talking" started later in life, with bull sessions among friends, "good and welfare" meetings in fraternities and sororities, and the like. Some conversations are straightforward and easy; they just seem to flow. ("Hi, I love your haircut. Where'd you get it? I'm looking for someone new to cut mine.") Other times they are so difficult you avoid having them for a long time, often *too long* a time. ("Honey, I think your dad may be losing his hearing. Have you noticed? He's e-mailing us rather than using the phone. And when we visit him and he's got the TV on, it's so loud it hurts my ears. What do you think we should do?")

The ease of most conversations falls somewhere between these two examples and are commonly more like this one: "I'm really hungry and there's nothing in the house that I want to eat. How do you feel about going out for a pizza?" Whether a particular conversation is simple or complex, whether you jump right in or wait for the "right moment," you'll feel better about the result if the conversation includes several practical features.

ELEMENTS OF EFFECTIVE COMMUNICATION

Where to Start Your Conversation

In general, before you start a conversation you have a conscious thought that you want to speak about to someone. Your thought may or may not require a preamble. If it seems to you that it does, you prepare one as best you can.

Through the decades, we have heard men admit that the most dreaded preamble to a conversation initiated by a woman begins with the words "We have to talk. . . ." A more enticing preamble to the same unexpected topic would be: "I've been thinking about our computer system. Can you make time for us to talk about it this weekend?"

With or without a preamble, it's useful to begin your conversation talking about yourself, not the other person. Conversations that begin with the word *you* tend to cause almost total loss of hearing on the part of the Listener: "You look like something's wrong, and you haven't said much all through dinner. You've been like this since you got home from your mother's house. What's going on with your mother that I don't know about?"

"I" statements are far more effective in capturing the attention of your conversation partner: "I've been worried ever since you got back from your mom's. Is everything okay? I get the sense you're concerned about something, and I'm wondering if you'd be willing to talk about what's going on."

When you respect yourself and your conversation partner sufficiently, you realize that your "expertise" is limited to yourself, not to someone else, no matter how close you are. Sometimes that's very hard to accept! But when you speak from your expertise, when you use "I" statements, your outcome will be a better communication.

How You Listen

I don't believe in mind reading. I do believe in listening carefully, which includes checking to see if you've accurately understood the words you've purportedly been listening to. The phrase, "I heard you say . . ." followed by

"Did I get that right?" is often useful to both partners in the conversation. In the case of your end-of-life conversations, an example might be:

Initiator: "I'm in perfectly good health. I've got some interesting travel plans as well as a new business opportunity, but before I take off in those directions, I'd like to talk with you about some more personal stuff. Can we make a date for lunch sometime next week?"

Listener: "I heard you say that you're healthy and busy, but there's some personal stuff you want to go over with me. Did I get that right?"

This particular conversation might end with a head nod or a spoken "Yes" or the Listener might add a specific piece of information, such as, "I'd like to do this as soon as possible. I'm a bit anxious to know what it is you have on your mind."

In an ideal world, this Initiator wouldn't have spoken until he or she knew all the components of the proposed conversation and could agree to an almost immediate lunch plan. In a less than ideal world, the Initiator would need to take a few more days to prepare, and the Listener would have to tolerate the anxiety if that wasn't too challenging.

Facing Sensitive Issues with Good Humor

We know that humor is important in life, and it is especially valuable as a component of healthy aging. Laughter, in fact, helps eliminate some of the conventions that keep us from talking about getting older and facing ourselves,

---

Not Entirely a Laughing Matter

When I began leading groups at a Connecticut senior center, the first week's homework was to find at least one joke, cartoon, quotation, or quip about aging . . . something that we could laugh about together. These are the only two items I received from a group of eleven participants, and the difference in their perspectives is funny in itself:

- "I was thinking about today's status symbols. The most ubiquitous is the cell phone; everyone has one clipped somewhere—onto their belts or in hip pockets, or even in their hands. I can't afford one (and if I could, I wouldn't know how to use it!). So I'm wearing my TV remote instead."

- "My gravestone must have engraved on it every one of my passwords. You never know who'll try to reach you, and what might work!"

our friends and family, and the aging process itself. Denial is more common, though, despite the fact that it is *not* a good thing.

Laughter absolutely helps us break some of the taboos that might otherwise silence us. Too often, silence is less a helpful boundary-setting tool than an impediment to, or protection *against*, intimacy. *Good* humor, on the other hand, is a joining agent. In this context, good humor encourages us to be courageous enough to talk about getting older and to think about the considerations that matter to us when the time comes to activate our end-of-life decisions. Humor sweetens and universalizes facing one's self and acknowledging the aging processes going on *for* ourselves and *all around* us, frequently leaving us feeling vulnerable. Good humor is particularly helpful when it enables us to recognize, acknowledge, and (as gracefully as possible) accept our changes.

Shall We Laugh?

A keen sense of the absurd is considered an ingredient for succeeding in life in general, and I'd suggest that it comes in especially handy all through the aging process. Babies, who enthrall most people, certainly enlist our sense of the absurd as they eat, attempt to move around, and even begin verbalizing. We nonetheless rather easily find them darling, sweet, even clever. Adolescents, experimenting with styles and attitudes, can primarily depend on familial loyalty to see them as silly, funny even, but beloved. So it goes as we age, through the years of relationships and earning a living, until we, or people we love, reach the later stages of aging. Then, I ask you: *Where has all our good humor gone—just when we perhaps need it most?* It would be a good idea to loosen up about aging and to channel good humor (kind laughter) as easily as we often channel anger throughout life. A tall order in some cases, I grant you.

Good humor increases goodwill. Sarcasm and vitriolic humor do just the opposite. When you are planning to tell or make a joke, be sure you can tell the difference between these qualities. When you're in doubt, take a look at your material. Are *you* going to be the object of the laughter? Then it's probably fine to proceed. If someone else is, this may not be *good* humor and is best avoided. Put-downs and mockery are mean, not funny. What they communicate isn't love or friendship or understanding, but derision and fear. You don't need to traffic in either of the latter qualities, particularly when your goal is good communication in the course of a conversation about end-of-life matters.

Laughter, especially if it provokes reminiscence and mutual memories—whether from childhood, high school, college, or any other times in your life, adds connection as a response to a conversation. See if you can elicit the experience of "Ah, yes, I remember it well!" through good humor, in your conversation.

Harold's Experience with Good Humor

Here we have an example of mingling warm humor successfully with mutual memories. Just before his sixty-fifth birthday, Harold determined to ask his younger sister (age sixty-two) to be the Listener to his end-of-life matters. He was afraid she'd say no, that she was too busy to take on another responsibility. So he began his request to her, by telephone, asking, "Do you remember when we were kids and you used to creep out the bedroom window at night to go smoke a cigarette with your friends, and I always covered for you with Mom and Dad?" (Indeed she remembered that, and they laughed together about other pranks, too.) Then Harold continued, "Well, the time has come when I need to ask you a favor in return! I'm fine, nothing to worry about, but can we get together to talk one day this week?" They were connected through the humorous memories, and her immediate answer was, "Sure; when?"

GROUNDWORK: SIX KEY QUESTIONS TO GUIDE YOUR CONVERSATION'S PREPARATION

I was a journalist before I was a therapist. To this day, whether I'm writing or teaching or, as with a book, doing both, I rely on the six key questions that journalists, when I was in graduate school, were taught to answer in their writing: **Who?**, **What?**, **Why?**, **How?**, **Where?**, and **When?**.

In thinking and talking and teaching about end-of-life matters, I rely on all six questions to help each Initiator focus on preparing aspects of what he or she wants to say. You'll read about all six of the questions in this book. Each question guides you through a discrete stage of the preparation, as developed in the chapters that follow. As Initiator, once you answer all six of these questions, you will have a framework for, and the content of, your conversation. You will have identified one or more Listeners and finished the planning. You will be ready and able to initiate your own conversation. As a kind of bonus, you'll also have read about personal Legacy Documents and be able to rule those in or out of your planning as well.

SUCCESSFUL CONVERSATIONS

Using the six key questions we just mentioned, **Who?**, **What?**, **Why?**, **How?**, **Where?**, and **When?**, as a framework for your preparations is by no means the only way to carry out a successful end-of-life conversation. Nevertheless, my reliance on this model is based on many people's experiences in conducting conversations that worked out well. Which brings up an important question: *How will you know if your discussion "worked out well"?* While each person must make that determination for herself or himself, I suggest the following four criteria to help you recognize success:

1. As Initiator, you are satisfied that each element of your wishes has been identified and discussed as needed.
2. Your Listener can accurately express an understanding of what your wishes are.
3. Your Listener specifically and clearly expresses a willingness to carry out your wishes.
4. Both you and your Listener get back to the primary task of living your lives well, without anxiety about what will happen at your end of life. You also both recognize that it's likely you won't know *when* your life will end very much in advance, if at all.

Think back to my story in chapter 1 about my parents' taboo-breaking telephone call. I, as the Listener, had no warning before their telephone call began that a conversation was coming, and admittedly, receiving that telephone call caused me anxiety. Even so, both my parents and I considered the conversation successful. They described what they wanted clearly and fully, so I understood their wishes, and they knew that I was willing to comply. Once that was agreed upon, we all went about our lives in an ordinary fashion until the moment came eight years later for me to recall and carry out my mother's wishes.

How Do You Recognize Successes?

As you read and work with the following nine chapters, another question may come to mind: *Who decides if, or when, each of the six questions has been answered satisfactorily?* I believe that each person is his or her own expert on this and decides the answer independently as Joan's mother demonstrates in the story that follows.

A Simple Matter of Jewelry

Joan's parents had chosen her to be their Listener and initiated a lengthy, thorough conversation with her about their end-of-life matters almost seven years before that became relevant, with her father's death. What he had wanted was therefore clear to his survivors, and it was easy enough for them to act according to his wishes. Just a few days after her husband's funeral,

One Conversation or More?

Throughout this book, I refer to "your conversation" or "the conversation" in the singular. However, it isn't inevitable or even essential that communicating your end-of-life wishes will be a onetime event. In some instances, as with my parents, once truly is enough. Alternatively, an event such as a funeral may trigger a discussion of your own funeral plans, but your other matters might remain to be discussed in a second or even third conversation. With this book as your guide, the process works as follows:

- First, think about the end of your life and **Who?** the best candidate is to know what your thoughts and wishes are.
- Second, think about **What?** information (the pertinent details) you want to share with someone you trust.
- Third, take the time you need to consider **Why?**, **How?**, and **Where?** you'll hold your conversation.
- Fourth, do it! **When?** Right away! Once you have answers to the first five key questions, "right away" is indeed the best answer to question six, "**When?**." Take the time you need, talking together one time or more, to reach the satisfying understanding and agreement about your end-of-life wishes that you are seeking.

Joan's mother initiated one further conversation with Joan. Mom expressed her recognition and concern that she hadn't been sufficiently clear about the way she wanted her jewelry distributed among her two daughters and several cousins, and she felt the need to review and clarify her wishes. Joan was grateful to have this information; she knew it would be enormously helpful in the future, and she was happy to make notes and repeat these wishes back to her mother, thus reassuring her.

What We Can Learn

We see a number of points explicit in this brief, successful story. First, of course, Joan's mom was the expert on her own wishes and recognized that. By clarifying those wishes, she removed the burden of "assuming or guessing" from Joan as well as from other family members. Second, through her action to revise the original conversation, Mom was reaffirming her decision to have Joan be the Listener of her wishes. Third, Joan was removing any "illusions" and instead putting reassuring facts into place, as she repeated back to Mom her clarifying wishes about the jewelry distribution at this conversation's conclusion.

In the case of a conversation about end-of-life matters, each prospective Initiator holds the key to what is best to say and to do in her or his own unique situation. I want to make clear to you that as you read each chapter and participate in the exercises, you will be making your own independent, individual choices about how to use the presented material for your personal goals in each conversation. You are in charge of the success of these decisions of yours; no one else is.

Responsible health-care practitioners, therapists, and physicians alike can guide people and offer examples or stories to clarify their guidance. Their first responsibility, however, is to encourage and allow each individual to make the unique choices and decisions that best fit his or her own temperament and situation. Not anyone else's.

COMMUNICATING IN SPECIAL CIRCUMSTANCES

What About Siblings?

I'm an only child, and I find myself puzzled sometimes about sibling rivalries that continue beyond childhood. However, they do exist, and I am aware that sibling-related issues are apt to be thorny and to relentlessly outlast many of the likely sibling benefits. Sometimes all the siblings in a family are chosen equally as the Listeners of a parent's conversation about end-of-life matters, but that is not always the case, or desirable. Children as well as parents can be honest and recognize the different strengths and personalities in their family members. One father I know chose to make his more geographically distant child the Listener of his end-of-life matters because, he described, "She's our sweeter child, and she'll be kinder to me than her sister." As in this dad's case, sometimes a parent prefers not to treat "the children" as a single unit, despite the fact that doing so may hurt the feelings of the child who is not asked to be the Listener. In other words, a "less sweet" child has feelings, too. When you ask yourself **Who?** you'd like to designate as Listener, I suspect you'll think back to these comments.

What Kind of Child Were You? An Exercise

But before we go to your conversation, try thinking for a minute of yourself as a child in your family of origin. Are you an *only* child in that context? Or do you have one or more siblings? If you have siblings, where do you fit in the family—oldest, youngest, in the middle? How many boys and how many girls are in your family? Has everyone lived to adulthood, or have any of your siblings died already? Any other details about your original family you'd like to give some thought to?

What Kind of Adult Are You?

Next, think of yourself as an adult. Are you a single adult or part of a couple? If you are a parent, do you have one child or more than one? Do you have nieces or nephews, godchildren, or others with whom you are close? Can you note, in your journal, just one or two sentences that describe you today? For example:

1. I am an only child who married and then had two sons. At this point in my life, I also have two daughters-in-law and five grandchildren, three boys and two girls, all in elementary school.
2. I am the elder of two children in my family of origin; my younger sister is very close to me. As an adult, I am the single (divorced) father of three: two boys and one girl, all college graduates now.

This very brief exercise gives you a multidimensional picture of yourself, both as a child and as an adult. It also helps you recognize that everyone, yourself included, has strengths as well as weaknesses. As an Initiator, you will be assessing to the best of your ability the qualities in your conversation's Listener that you find important. Your choice of Listener will be based on *your assessment* of your needs and the best candidate to meet them.

To protect against future disagreements or controversy after a conversation has been held, parents of two or more children might consider a few options, which are apt to also be used effectively by families of an only child. Audio recordings can help preserve the accuracy of a verbal conversation. Alternatively, a Listener might choose to resort to a more tedious option: to take notes and read them aloud so they can be signed off on by the Initiator as well as by anyone else present for the conversation. As you may remember, my father suggested that I take notes as we spoke, and I'd already begun doing that. It was important to both of us that this information be preserved accurately.

A SIBLING STORY

One set of brothers, Arthur and Howard, adults now in their fifties, had parents who were becoming elderly and frail, Mom more so than Dad. One of the sons, Howard, was divorced and lived alone in an apartment in a town near his parents' home. The other son, Arthur, was married and lived in a different state. It would be logical, you might think, for Howard, the son living nearby, to notice the changes in their parents and begin to do something about broaching this subject to them. Wrong. His sense was that these were his mom and dad; they'd always made the rules. He'd just continue with that pattern, and Arthur should do the same thing.

Arthur, the younger and more geographically distant son, however, was concerned by this lack of communication with his aging parents and came to see me about becoming the Initiator of a talk with them, despite Howard's virtually opposite point of view. At this writing, Arthur is gathering information from his father about the couple's physicians, their attorney, safe deposit box, and so forth, and has chosen not to involve Howard in the process. Being siblings, even close in age and of the same gender, does not mean having identical personalities, needs, wishes, or perceptions. That's an important fact for siblings, as well as for parents themselves, to know and accept as they lay the groundwork for a conversation. It's particularly important to consider when you read the material in chapter 4, where you will be considering **Who?** to choose as *your* conversation's Listener.

When You're a Twin (or Another Multiple)

Multiples (twins, triplets, quadruplets, etc.) are more common in the twenty-first century than in previous eras and deserve some brief, special consideration. Twins are the most frequently occurring multiple, and so we'll focus on them. Twins carry a burden separate from those of singleton siblings. Parents often expect a unique closeness between them and for them to be best friends—forever. That's a burden for many twins and an expectation that can stunt the love that might otherwise grow naturally between them. Like their singleton siblings, twins do not necessarily grow up with identical or even parallel views of their family or experiences in that family, or much else for that matter. So when the time comes for parents of multiples to initiate their conversation about end-of-life matters, they will find themselves in the same boat as all other parents in choosing a Listener. As I'll discuss in chapter 4, whether you're the parent of one adult child or adult triplets, you need to know what your needs are and do your best to assess who is most likely to be able to say and mean, *"Yes, I am willing and able to carry out your wishes."* That's your first choice of Listener.

When You Play Both Roles

The story of Arthur and Howard above brings to mind still another special circumstance that some of you may face. Although it is by no means the only reason, the growing number of people with dementia makes it ever more likely that you will need first to have a hand in initiating a conversation and then becoming its Listener. Unlike those who initiate their own conversations because they can and do acknowledge that *"someday* I will die," initiating a conversation on behalf of someone else—who is facing extended, severe disability rather than imminent death, and who hasn't yet made the conscious decision to act on his or her own—significantly increases the difficulty. Tony's story brings to life this very situation.

Tony's Story: One Sibling's Example

Tony, one of my patients, was one of three sons in an Italian Catholic family. As the only child living near his parents and sensing that his father's dementia was increasingly impairing his decision making, Tony decided to initiate an end-of-life conversation with his parents. Primarily, he was afraid of making a mistake if he didn't find out in advance what they'd want *"when the time came,"* as he put it very gently and carefully to them. What Tony really wanted to find out was whether they wanted to be buried or cremated, so he wouldn't be left without information and inadvertently make the wrong choice. After initiating a first meeting, however, he found himself still clueless, but now his parents were mad at him for *"poking around in our business."* He was appalled and came to me for some guidance.

We recognized that his mother was furious because his talking with them made it much harder for her to continue her intense denial of her husband's deteriorating condition. Her stance was protective—of both of them. Tony's questions left her feeling at a new disadvantage.

His dad, on the other hand, was actually grateful that his son seemed to be willing to take care of them both, to take on the job he'd been trying to carry out with increasing struggles and even failures. For example, he'd wander out of the house and panic. Where was he and how would he get back home? He welcomed Tony's questions as interventions that would help keep him safe at the same time that his wife resisted, struggling to keep up appearances of independence for each of them.

As we talked, Tony began to sense that he had waited too long to get involved, and he was at a loss how to proceed. Ultimately, he and his dad had a lucid, brief, private conversation, during which Tony posed many questions; his dad responded. Tony accepted as fact everything his dad said he wanted. Tony is now planning a separate conversation with his mother, and he thinks that she will become more accepting of it as she adjusts to having help in the house so that her husband is safe, and she also is less responsible for "everything."

When You're Part of a Blended Family

Not all divorced people remain alone for the rest of their lives. Many form new, significant relationships, in or outside of marriage. In the course of merging or remarrying, as with the Brady Bunch on television years ago, blended families develop. Emily, a woman with two sons, fell in love with, married, and moved in with Harold and his daughter. They immediately became a blended family of five. Just how much fun do you think that was?

Well, it may ultimately develop into fun, with careful engineering of bedtimes, bathrooms, closets, furniture, and such. But then there will be colleges and careers, choices of marrying, living together, or not coupling, either by choice or default—and the successful parents of this blended group will gradually age. Whenever they feel it is the right time, *what* do they do about having a constructive conversation?

In some families, we see reversion to the pre-blended situations. In the case of Harold and Emily, he decided to talk first to his wife and then to his daughter. Emily, after her conversation with her husband, got her boys together and talked with them about her own matters. For both Harold and Emily, this "divide and conquer" conversation process worked out just fine.

Acknowledge Your Family's Conversation Heritage

In her graphic memoir *Can't We Talk About Something More Pleasant?* American cartoonist Roz Chast uses humor and illustrations to portray her efforts to help her parents navigate many of their end-of-life issues. She begins her book with a euphemistic dialogue in which she, as an adult only child, asks her parents if they ever "think about THINGS?" Frantic, she tells them that she has "no idea what you guys WANT" in case "something HAPPENED." As her parents crack up laughing, she seems to wonder whether she might be the only sane person in the conversation, in the room, or perhaps in the family.

The way we deal with issues such as the end of life is strongly influenced by habits of communication (or lack of it) within the families we grow up in, what family therapists speak of as your "family of origin." Revealing and understanding this influence is valuable, especially if you want or need to address end-of-life issues in a manner that breaks with family tradition.

An Exercise about Your Own Communication Heritage, Part 1

The following writing prompts are designed to help you explore your family's "communication heritage." Take no more than twenty-five minutes to look at and respond in your journal to some or all of them.

1. In your childhood home, how was conversation about anyone's dying and death engaged in? Was it considered an acceptable topic of conversation, or was it something to be whispered about or even ignored? Or something else? Were children included or excluded both in conversations and in attending the funeral when a relative or close family friend died? Was death a subject children were free to talk about and process in your childhood home, or in your home of procreation, or was it a mysterious, perhaps frightening, taboo topic for children?

2. In the family of your adult life, is death a forbidden topic of discussion, acceptable, a welcome one, or something else entirely?

3. Is death a subject you're "allowed" to think about and perhaps mention, or are you only expected to worry about death in silence, and deny it?

4. Who makes these rules for you today?

5. What is the comfort level, in your current family, for talking about love, illness, and death?

6. What about your comfort with conversations about possessions, money, spiritual beliefs, and values?

7. In both your family and your friendship circle, which of the above topics is everyday conversation material, which is taboo, and which do you talk about only on rare occasions?

Be sure to make notes about your thoughts and responses to all seven questions in your journal! Your answers will help you recognize aspects of your family of origin as well as your family as an adult, and your roles in each. No behaviors are required to remain static. You are welcome to make changes when you see opportunities for improving your habits and actions.

An Exercise about Your Own Communication Heritage, Part 2

As you have considered your own family's communication heritage in this exercise, it's possible that either you respect it and want to continue the traditions, or you recognize that there are habits you'd like to change in order to improve the ways you communicate with one another. This is good information for you to have processed and to put to use as you grapple with a conversation of your own in many of the following chapters.

For those of you who envision changes you'd like to make in the communication rules or habits in your current life, give yourself some time to journal about this as well.

1. What about the communication habits and rules in your life would you like to change?
2. How would you like to make the change(s)?
3. Is there anything else to note or reflect on?

Before we move on to the specifics of setting up your end-of-life conversation, there's one more task for you to consider while we're laying the groundwork for it. We'll turn our attention now to some thoughts about just what you would like to accomplish *before* you devise the conversation about *your* wishes for the end of your life.

A BUCKET LIST AS A PRECURSOR
TO YOUR CONVERSATION

As we will discuss in chapter 5, "Ask Yourself, What?," your end-of-life matters encompass significantly more than simply funeral preferences. What happens with your considerations at that point in your life reflects how you've lived your life, the values and beliefs you have held and very likely still hold, the goals you have set, and those you have accomplished.

One way to act on your values and set goals that are worthwhile to you is to develop what is commonly known as a *bucket list*, an expression that arises from the phrase *to kick the bucket*, a euphemism for *to die*. In a popular 2007 movie, *The Bucket List*, an actual bucket list generates a fair amount of controversy, as may happen in real life. In part, this relates to the desire many people have to deny that we need or want anything like a bucket list and to deny the personal need to plan ahead "in case of" dying.

Whether you consider these lists ridiculous or insightful, please take some time to use the following exercises to generate a list of your own. If you already have some items on a bucket list, review them in light of the following questions, and add or subtract items as appropriate.

Exercise: Create Your Bucket List, Part 1

In some of the communication groups I work with, we begin by creating a *group* bucket list. For instance, one group's list included:

- Talk about sensitive end-of-life issues with my spouse or life partner.
- Get long-term care insurance for my wife and myself.
- See at least two of our national parks.
- Lose twenty pounds.
- Let my hair come in gray.
- Teach my husband to balance the checkbook and use accounting software.
- Make sure my grandchildren know I love them.
- Eat at one of the world's best restaurants.

None of these items may interest you, of course, but you get the idea. In this first exercise, you'll focus on things you'd like to do in the relative short term, roughly within the next decade.

I found it hard to get into bucket lists—until one of my sons-in-law told me we were going on a trip for my next birthday and wanted to know where I'd like to go—what cities were on my bucket list? "None" didn't seem like a good answer so I started to think. Suddenly, I was able to create a bucket list including five cities I'd love to get to: Venice, Florence, Sydney, Positano or Sicily, and Vancouver. While we ultimately toured through Wales for countryside and hikes and London for theater instead, I'd begun my bucket list, and it continues to this day—although I rarely talk—or think—about it. Since you don't have my son-in-law to prompt you, here are some questions that might help you create a bucket list of your own:

1. What is your next milestone birthday (e.g., will you turn 30, 45, 50, 65, or 70, etc.)?
2. At your last milestone birthday, did you mark the event in a special way? If not, why not?
3. Whichever decade is your next one, consider whether you have some thing(s) specific in mind to (a) mark the completion of your current decade or (b) mark your entrance into the new decade.
4. What are the experiences you'd like to have before your next milestone birthday? Are there things you are waiting to do as a treat for yourself when that birthday occurs?
5. Is there anything else you have in mind to do either before or after the start of your next decade? For example, at dinner one night,

a colleague of mine showed me a jewelry pouch, shyly but with pride. From it, she removed a fabulous pair of gold and jeweled earrings that she'd had copied from a museum collection.

   a. "I'd never have done this but for the bucket list you talked about," she announced. "It seemed way too expensive for my lifestyle. But then, I was having a big birthday and not sure how to celebrate it, and I thought: bucket list! So I photographed them from the museum case, commissioned a jeweler to make earrings like the photo, and now I have them to wear."

   b. Her smile was all the validation I needed for encouraging as many other people as possible, including you, to develop a bucket list, too.

6. Allow yourself to take the time now to let a plan emerge for the next decade you will embark upon. Once you've outlined the details, consider the following additional questions:

   a. Is there anyone with whom you are willing to share these thoughts and plans? When and how will you make this happen?

   b. If there is someone, have you considered this person as a candidate for being the Listener to your end-of-life matters? If appropriate, have you ruled him or her out or is he or she currently still under consideration?

Exercise: Create Your Bucket List, Part 2

Now let's expand your dreams, goals, and plans throughout the rest of your life.

1. Take ten minutes to think personally about your own bucket list items, and keep thinking after you initially feel you've finished. Make this list in your journal as ideas pop into your head. You can easily cross off or add items as you go.

2. Write about the things you'd especially like to do before your life ends. Some of you will have more decades ahead of you, and some fewer. Neither situation needs to stop you. Just let yourself imagine, fantasize, play! This part of your list is meant to include all the Big Treats. These are the things you haven't done yet because they are too expensive, too frivolous, or for whatever other reason keeps you from doing them. Just write them down.

3. What things, big or little, do you really care about having accomplished, seen, or owned in your lifetime? Is there something, big or small, within your control that you don't want to have missed out on during your life? These are some of the things a bucket list is made of. Make a note about them for yourself.

For me, this last set of questions was especially provocative. I'd spent over twenty years living simultaneously in Westport, Connecticut, and Manhattan. The commute had become drudgery, and as anyone who's done this will know, the shoes or shirt I wanted to wear were *always* in my closet in the other city. I determined that I wanted to give a try to living and working exclusively in one place, and I chose Manhattan. In 2016, I crossed that item off my bucket list when I moved into the city full-time! I think of it as *my* bucket list experiment, and it really pleases me to have recognized it, and then acted on it.

Go ahead and create a bucket list for yourself now. Please give it a try, even if you think a bucket list is ridiculous or that the expression has been overused and wasn't so good to begin with, either. This was Frank's view. He was a participant in one of my groups. He was initially quite annoyed by the phrase *bucket list* and didn't hesitate to say so. Frank ultimately wrote a long and interesting list of things he'd spent his adult life denying himself because they cost too much or were frivolous, and so on. Frank liked his list and, to my knowledge, has already done at least two things on it: he's writing the book he'd previously postponed getting around to, and he's attending a writer's workshop in a part of the United States he'd never been to before and had a yen to see. You can let this bucket-list exercise take you anywhere you want, literally as well as figuratively!

Here, in chapter 3, not only have you been introduced to and worked on your bucket list, but you have also discovered the six key questions you will address in planning your own conversation: **Who?**, **What?**, **Why?**, **How?**, **Where?**, and **When?**. In addition, we've considered some of the many varieties of families that exist and the differences between them as we lay the groundwork for initiating an end-of-life conversation. As you read further in this book, you will have the opportunity, first, to identify your own role as either Initiator or Listener of a conversation with end-of-life considerations, and second, to look specifically at each of the six questions. In chapter 4, the first of the questions to be considered is **Who?**. I think **Who?** is the most important question to answer because it provides the context for how you will focus your answers to the rest of the key questions.

4

Ask Yourself, Who?

The single biggest problem in communication is the illusion that
it has taken place.

—George Bernard Shaw, Irish Dramatist (1856–1950)

TRUE CONFESSIONS

*A*fter I had thought and talked about the concept for this book, and
spent time outlining my ideas for it, I presented the premise to a meeting
of colleagues, who were fascinated. They found it compelling and were appreciative, so I moved forward, continuing to teach and write this material.
Something seemed missing, though. And then I had that "aha" moment.
In a conversation with my agent, she told me candidly that I needed to go
even further. I had to let the book become more personal, despite my inner-
therapist's reluctance to disclose! She emphatically "suggested" that I follow
my own outline and check out my personal thoughts and wishes before I did
any more of the work to revise the book. She not only intended to *encourage*
me to initiate a conversation about my own end-of-life matters, but basically,
she said I *had* to do it, and then to include some of my experiences as Initiator, not just as Listener, in the book.

Oh, really? I thought to myself, bristling. Why wasn't it going to be
enough for me to simply rely on my experience as the Listener of a conversation and teach from that perspective? Did I really need to push myself to go
still further and initiate one of my own? Must I, now, do for myself exactly
what my parents had done, *and what I am telling you readers is so important*

and valuable? I can't just sit here as a mostly blank screen, a Listener, and guide you through being an Initiator of this process?

The therapist in me began to fight with the writer, but in the long run, I am happy to tell you, the writer won. (Making me, I suspect, an even better therapist.) I released the therapist's conventional premise that being a blank screen allows your caseload to picture you as they wish to, without any of your real-life foibles being visible, and thus enhances the benefits of the treatment. I began a new step for myself in communicating. I've allowed myself to be visible as a woman with personal experiences and feelings here. The results are recognizable in bits and pieces throughout this book. You may already have noticed some of this as you've been reading.

LET'S TALK ABOUT **WHO?**

As you know from reading the end of chapter 3, it's important to select a **Who?** right up front. So I did. With ease actually, as my parents had been able to do. My **Who?** was to be both of my daughters, adults now, married, and parents of young children. Initially, I had considered having my **Who?** include not only my daughters but also their husbands, my sons-in-law, whom I also love and trust. Ultimately, I decided to limit the group to "the girls," keeping it small and, I hoped, simple.

The choice of my daughters was so obvious to me that I really didn't have to spend a lot of time thinking about options. I trust them, and the primary issue I think we face is geography. Neither lives very close to me, although one lives within an hour from my home, and that's just going to have to be good enough. Another issue is that they are parents of children who were then very young. I decided to gamble on this one, and trusted that I'd survive until the youngest ones were in school for full days. Writing the book took long enough that the youngest pair has just turned seven, so this gamble has already paid off.

I'll tell you more about my own thoughts and feelings as they seem relevant. For now, let's explore how you'll select your own **Who?**—that is, the Listener(s) of *your* conversation about your own end-of-life matters.

CHOOSING YOUR **WHO?**

When you spend time deciding to have or not to have a particular conversation, and when it's important enough to you that you decide *to have it* and actually want to plan it out carefully, before initiating it, you recognize that the conversation matters to you so much that you want to be sure you "do it right." You want to do everything you can think of to be sure that you will be satisfied with its outcome. This is especially true with sensitive topics such as end-of-life considerations. *You become aware of how important it is for you to know that ultimately the person or people with whom you've been talking fully understand what you are saying to them, what you are asking of them.*

In planning a successful conversation, therefore, **Who?** you will be talking to is of the utmost importance. As we begin now to look at the components of a successful end-of-life conversation, I recommend that your first consideration be *"**Who** shall I talk with about my wishes?"*

Many people will want to identify Listeners for two categories of end-of-life matters: general topics and health-care matters. Let's begin with our focus on the Listener who is not a health-care provider. I'll talk later in this chapter about trusted medical personnel.

For some people, as it was for me, the choice of Listener may be immediately obvious—a spouse or adult only child, for example. However, life is unpredictable. I urge anyone planning this conversation to complete the exercises in this chapter—if only to verify that your obvious choice is indeed the best one for you and to provide one or more alternatives, should your obvious first choice become unavailable. In my case, the mother-in-law of one of my daughters became seriously ill in another state a couple of weeks before our conversation had first been scheduled. Given the choice of proceeding without this daughter or waiting several months until the illness had been

---

The Grief Factor

Most of the time, your Listener is closely related or otherwise intimately connected to you. Therefore, it's important to recognize that, at the time of your illness and/or death, it's not just carrying out your end-of-life wishes that can weigh heavily on your Listener but also intense emotions—grief, shock, emotional pain, and loss. Having "all the answers" your conversation will provide truly helps a lot, but it doesn't in any way eliminate these intense feelings. I won't attempt to solve Listener sadness in this book, but I do want to acknowledge and validate it. It's something you may want to keep in the back of your mind as this process evolves or even talk about with a family therapist or another health-care professional, if warranted.

resolved, I chose the latter, without any regrets. But I know I was lucky in this respect, and this degree of flexibility may not be possible in every situation.

DEFINING YOUR CRITERIA FOR LISTENER QUALITIES

A Listener must fulfill two obligations: first, be willing and able to take part in the conversation and, second, be willing and able to fulfill the Initiator's wishes when the time comes. Carrying out these responsibilities calls for meeting certain criteria, which you determine, and demonstrating qualities you think are desirable. Some of the qualities I highlight below are likely to be valuable for nearly all end-of-life circumstances, while others will depend entirely on your specific wishes. Here are some examples of popular, widely desired qualities that you might include in your criteria:

- Integrity: Someone who is ethically sound, with a strong moral code; someone who believes a promise is a promise and can be counted on to act accordingly. A reliably honest person.
- Trustworthiness: Someone who is worthy of your confidence, preferably demonstrated by deeds you're familiar with.
- Affection and/or respect for you: Someone whose feelings will help reinforce his or her commitment to your wishes.
- Ingenuity/flexibility: A person who can adapt to changes in circumstances that may interfere with carrying out your wishes, yet be able to be true to their spirit if change is needed.
- Capability: Someone able to deal effectively with legal or health-care systems, cultural associations, government entities, and other organizations, depending on your wishes.
- Age and health: Relevant only insofar as they contribute to your Listener's likelihood of outliving you.

Exercise: Build on Your Habit of Trust

Learning to trust and to be able to assess other people fairly and accurately are skills that take practice. The following exercise will help you see your skills in light of past experience and be helpful to you as you consider **Who?** you will select as your Listener.

1. Think back to a situation in your life in which you had to find someone reliable and trustworthy, such as selecting a godparent, entrusting a secret, or finding a person to take care of someone or something

dear to you. Spend a few minutes visualizing before, during, and after you made your choice.

2. Now, briefly write your responses to the following questions in your journal:

   a. How did you choose the person you decided upon? Was your choice based on "gut" or some more specific criteria you were aware of?

   b. If you considered more than one person, what was the deciding factor?

   c. How did you get the information you needed to make your decision?

   d. Did the person you selected meet your expectations? If not, what if anything could you have done differently to improve the outcome?

3. In reviewing these questions and your answers, do you think you're becoming comfortable with your ability to select a Listener?

Of course, your selection criteria above may very well not be the only considerations in making your final choice of Listener. Circumstantial elements are likely to come into play, most often family dynamics. The situation of a parent with more than one adult child is just such an element, although, as I've mentioned, flexibility can often help you work through some of these issues.

FOR PARENTS WITH ADULT CHILDREN

If you are a parent without a spouse who could serve as a viable Listener, choosing one of your adult children may seem an appropriate alternative. How and when do you announce or explain your choice to the children you have not asked to be your Listener? For some people, an addendum or letter attached to their Last Will and Testament does the job. By the time it's become public, you are not going to be there to be yelled at, which might feel like an added benefit. *"The children will have to work it out without me"* is the premise. I'm not comfortable with that thinking, but frankly, I have heard from many people that they seriously are.

Other parents may be uncomfortable putting one child in the position of Listener, only to be recognized as such by siblings *after* the parent's death. Not surprisingly, this child may balk at going along with such a plan and either refuse to be the Listener or insist that the other sibling(s) be involved.

Some parents I've worked with ultimately chose to write an explanation to the other children almost immediately after talking with *one*. This is to clear the air and prevent hard feelings, but not to open the discussion. (This doesn't always turn out well, by the way. Family members do harbor feelings, especially the darker feelings that being left out of this choice might stimulate.)

Still other Initiators can't tolerate this tension and prefer to invite all the children to participate as Listeners. These Initiators may find themselves facing tensions of a very different sort, one of which can be having to keep the children from disagreeing and fighting with each other before, during, and after your conversation.

When you are dealing with issues and questions regarding multiple children, it's really preferable that you not create trouble in the family by appearing to *favor* one child over another. Select your **Who?** accordingly, if at all possible. Clearly state the name of your chosen Listener to prevent either guesses or negative sibling reactions later. At the very least, explain your choice when you recognize it is appropriate, or when your Listener guides you to speak about it. For the sake of your family, I encourage you to prevent creating hard feelings unnecessarily or thoughtlessly.

One Couple's Creative Solution

Ed and Jenny, a couple in their early eighties, attended one of my conversation workshops. They had been married to each other for eight years, since the end of their previous marriages, and they both had children from those first unions. Ed and Jenny had become a couple that was loving and independent, and they were both very anxious that when one of them died, there be no "seedy behaviors" on the part of any of their children.

In terms of the end-of-life matters conversation, initially their plan was to talk with one another (i.e., the spouse would be the **Who?**). They each trusted that the surviving spouse would do the right things, per their conversations. They pictured that, when the first death occurred, things would go smoothly. But what would the surviving spouse be left to deal with? Would jealousies develop between the biological children and the surviving spouse?

Four weeks into the six-week workshop, the couple came up with a plan that seemed to fit their needs. They each would talk with their spouse and one child from their first marriage. That child was to be the "designated replacement." Jenny and Ed had created a way to cover all the bases without being able to see into the future. They'd created a method that provided a sense of safety for each of them. Their **Who?** was resolved creatively and without further issues as far as they could predict. They each trusted that the surviving spouse would carry out their wishes, and the existence of a "designated replacement" provided a fail-safe guarantee of this.

LISTENERS OUTSIDE OF YOUR IMMEDIATE FAMILY

Frequently, **Who?** might best be answered by designating a friend, co-worker, member of the clergy, or a more distant relative than a spouse or child. The qualities you would look for would be much the same as those for your immediate family member: preferably someone younger than yourself, whom you trust and know well and who is willing to take on this responsibility.

If you've already named a health-care proxy, let me state the obvious. He or she *can* be chosen to be the Listener to your end-of-life conversation, but there is no requirement that this be the case. You may also want to consider talking with an estate attorney, financial advisor, or other professional with whom you have already established a trusting relationship, to see if he or she would be willing to become your conversation's Listener.

Reach Out to Find a Listener

Finding candidates beyond your immediate family may take more than a superficial effort. I'm thinking of a participant in a conversation workshop, a lively, well-educated professional man of eighty-five who had divorced, now considered himself single, and was working part-time. His two adult children each lived more than a thousand miles from him and rarely called. He described them as "difficult," and when I asked how he thought they might describe him, he said, "Distant . . . uncaring."

He then announced, "I'm totally alone, and really, no one cares. So who the Hell could I have this conversation with, if I even knew what I wanted to say in it?"

Tough questions. His resolution? After some prodding, he remembered a cousin who was fifteen years his junior and whom he'd mentored in her business career many years earlier. They'd stayed in touch annually via holiday cards, and he knew how to reach her by telephone. So he called her. Within two weeks, they'd met, and she'd agreed to become the Listener of his conversation and to follow through with all of his end-of-life matters whenever he was ready to talk about them with her. In fact, she said that she was "awfully glad" he'd told her about the conversation because she suspected her own father and mother ought to be having one with her as well. She was going to think about *initiating* one with them.

This story exemplifies how creativity and thought may not only get you what you need, but in the process, you might be educating, and thus helping, someone else. Never say never!

EXERCISE: ASSESS YOUR CANDIDATES

As some of the stories in this book reveal, the most *obvious* choice for your **Who?** to choose as Listener may not be the best candidate. This exercise will help you identify your options.

1. List the criteria and personality traits that you will use to evaluate your candidates. In particular, do you anticipate fulfilling your end-of-life matters in areas that will call for specialized skills or knowledge (e.g., do you have an art or rare books collection that you want handled in a specific manner?)? If so, either be sure that your Listener *is* equipped to deal with that collection or name someone else who is suited to the task. Alternatively, if you so choose, you could set up a bequest, or you might even begin to divest yourself of those possessions while you're still in good health.
2. List the names and relationships of anyone in your immediate family (spouse, children, parents, siblings) who might be a candidate for your choice of **Who?** Review each candidate in view of your criteria, including personality traits and specialized skills. Remove from this list any individuals who don't qualify after some consideration.
3. Do you have anyone in your extended family (cousins, aunts, or uncles) who might be candidates? If so, list them and apply your criteria, as you've just done for your immediate family.
4. If you are still searching, take a look beyond your family to close friends, longtime coworkers, clergy, or professional advisors. Once again, list their names, assess their suitability, and narrow your field as you proceed.

When you are done, you are likely to have at least one candidate. If you have more, rank them from first to last choice. You'll begin by asking your first choice to be your Listener, but if he or she cannot say yes to you, you will be immediately prepared to approach your second candidate and so on.

THE NEED FOR FLEXIBILITY

Having more than one candidate for the Listener to your discussion of end-of-life matters gives you valuable flexibility as you start to make your plans for this conversation. So many events are likely to intervene between initial planning and the final carrying out of your wishes.

This was the case for Jimmy, a divorced man in his fifties with no children, from an Italian American family, whom I mentioned at the beginning of chapter 2. Despite having siblings who lived near his parents, Jimmy was the one who responded whenever his parents had problems. It turns out that it would have been hugely helpful if Jimmy had had a backup for his role. He took part in my conversation workshop in order to prepare to initiate a conversation with his parents, so he could be the Listener to their end-of-life matters. During the first four weeks, he was an active participant in every meeting. Jimmy initially worked out how he would approach the subject with his folks and then turned his attention to a series of questions he wanted them to answer for him. However, at week five, he was uncharacteristically quiet in the workshop, a behavior that signaled a problem. When asked directly about his silence, he spoke flatly, "I've got lung cancer. Stage four."

Jimmy's life had just been turned upside down. Instead of going ahead and initiating a conversation with his aging parents so that he could be their Listener, he suddenly had an imperative need for a conversation of his own. While intending to do everything he possibly could to restore his health, Jimmy needed simultaneously to think through the elements of the conversation, for which, of course, he would be the Initiator now, with his own list of wishes and personal information to be discussed. And what about that necessary conversation he wanted to help his parents initiate? At this point, Jimmy had absolutely no obvious answer to the key question **Who?** in either situation.

I tell this story to emphasize the fact that, with life and death, we just never know what will be next. We need to remember to think "on our feet" and that it is never too late to *revise* a plan.

YOUR HEALTH-CARE PROFESSIONAL AS LISTENER

Now that Medicare has decided to reimburse physicians for one time they spend with a patient discussing end-of-life options, wishes, actions to refuse, or potential locations of treatment (home care versus hospital care, palliative care, or hospice in a facility separate from the patient's home), it's important for you to consider identifying a medical person as still another Listener for your end-of-life matters. The discussions will be different, although the content—your **What?**—will, to some extent, be the same, as we'll discuss in the next chapter.

Age was mentioned as one of the considerations in choosing a Listener. The importance of age for a health-care-provider Listener will likely be less of an issue than it would be for more closely related Listeners. Your choice of a health-care professional whom you trust to discuss and follow your wishes is apt to be based on the individual's knowledge, professional experience, even reputation, and perhaps on subjects he or she has written or spoken about that are meaningful to you.

For example, Jo, a member of one of my groups, remarked that she assessed her health-care professionals on their ability to be vulnerable. She considered it essential that they be clearly able to appreciate and understand vulnerability in others, that is, in her, a patient.

"I'd never want to discuss my own end-of-life wishes, the dos and the don'ts, with anyone who I couldn't cry in front of," Jo began. "Yet one time, with a doctor, when I cried, they got very brusque and the conversation we were having ended abruptly. And that's only when I got upset about a thyroid diagnosis! I can hardly stand to imagine how awful that would be if I were talking about the end of my life. . . . Whew!"

Jo eventually chose to have this important conversation with her naturopath, instead of her internist, for this very reason. When asked, her naturopath agreed and therefore became Jo's medical Listener of choice. (I suggested to Jo that she check to see if her naturopath could be authorized to help provide her care if she became hospitalized. Naturopaths do not yet have privileges in most hospitals, I am told, although they are working to change that. This will be an important consideration.)

Exercise: Evaluate Your Providers

This exercise is designed to help you choose which of your own health-care providers you'd like to ask to talk with you about your end-of-life care.

1. Begin by making a list of the name, area of specialization, and office telephone number of each health-care provider you see at least once a year.
2. Make a note of how often you and this provider have office visits each week, month, or year.
3. Picture making an appointment for this conversation or, at the very least, have it be part of a telephone call. You want to know the answers to the following questions from a physician you are considering as your medical Listener:
   a. Does Dr. X participate in discussions with her patients about planning for end-of-life care?
   b. If yes, how often do these conversations get updated? ("Once a year or in the case of a new diagnosis of an illness" is the answer you'd prefer to hear.)

    c. If these discussions are not routine, ask why not? (It's possible there's a good reason, i.e., an alternate way of updating. Find that out.)

    d. This may be the most important question of all for many of you, in guiding your selection of a Listener who serves you as a health-care provider:

        i. Has Dr. X had a conversation of this sort with a family member or close friend, and with a colleague?

        ii. If the answer to this question is no, you very well may want to see if one is scheduled. If it is not, this may not matter to you at all. On the other hand, it might tell you that this health-care provider may not be the right person for you to talk with. I say this, in part, because of Jo's comments about a Listener's ability to be vulnerable—and also empathic. There are lots of people for whom it's hard to picture thinking and talking about end-of-life options with a health-care provider who hasn't already gone through this thought process for themselves and experienced the many vulnerable feelings, including anxiety, that it's apt to provoke. There are also many people for whom this is not a primary consideration. What's important isn't *to which group* you belong, but that you recognize what's important to you.

4. Slowly think through the information you've gathered. With whom do you believe you'll feel most comfortable having this discussion? That's your plan-A candidate. Identify your plan-B candidate, just in case you'll need one.

5. Call the plan-A provider and set up your appointment for the conversation, preferably within a week of making your call.

6. If necessary, immediately call your plan-B provider to schedule there, instead.

If, at this point in considering your personal and medical **Who?** you are still undecided, go ahead and make a provisional decision, and move on to the next chapter, where we will explore the **What?** of your conversation. Chapter 5, "Ask Yourself, What?," turns to a more concrete part of a conversation, and the information in it may also help you better picture who would be best as your Listener. Be sure to base your decision on concrete, factual information, not illusion. (If, of course, the **Who?** decision is one you've been able to make already, you are fully ready to move on and address the question **What?** in chapter 5.)

5

Ask Yourself, What?

> Good conversation is just as stimulating as black coffee, and just
> as hard to sleep after.

— Anne Morrow Lindbergh, American Writer (1906–2001)

At this point in your reading, it's very possible that you feel up to making
the decision to plan and actually have a conversation as the Initiator. What's
more, by now, many of you have already chosen the **Who?** of your conversation, your Listener(s). That's an important beginning decision!

I will *not* offer any sort of guidance either on writing a formal Last
Will and Testament or on if or how to write an advance care directive, living
will, and health-care proxy. If you choose to create any of these additional
documents to include in your communication about your end-of-life matters,
I encourage you to seek the help of specialized consultants, one example of
whom could be a trust and estate attorney.

Let's look at the options for materials that can be included as you consider **What?** you are likely to want to discuss with your Listener(s).

WHAT? DO I WANT TO BE SURE TO TELL MY LISTENER(S)?

When my parents initiated *our* conversation, they decided to talk with me
pretty much without any noticeable advance planning on their part. As you
may recall, friends of theirs had just described their own idea and plan, and my
parents said they liked the concept so much they decided to move forward to
initiate a conversation of their own with me, rather spontaneously, and almost
entirely unscripted. In their favor, of course, was the fact that my father was an

attorney, and he was fastidious in his personal record keeping and organization of files and information. My mother was also in business outside the house, and well organized. Therefore, when they adapted Al and Faye's idea for this conversation, it was easier for my parents to pull together all that was needed to run down a list of the important information that the **What?** of the conversation comprised than it might have been for many other people. My parents were working without the electronic devices the majority of us now take for granted. Most of the needed information is at our fingertips (literally) in our cell phones and computers, and easily transmitted. We're very lucky.

SCARING YOUR LISTENER IS NOT YOUR GOAL

Thinking back, I remember vividly how my personal confusion and anxiety, as well as concern about their well-being, all were growing while my parents and I were talking on the telephone. It almost goes without saying that once my mother specifically articulated their first question to me, "*When we die, are you going to want a funeral or a memorial service, or what?*," I panicked.

"WHAT are you trying to tell me?" I demanded, frightened and very perplexed. My folks were focused on the facts they wanted to bring to my attention. They'd given no thought at all to how I might be feeling, suddenly immersed in all of this.

Based on common sense plus my firsthand experience as a Listener, I strongly recommend that, as Initiators, *you* do your very best to protect your Listener(s) from an unnecessarily frightening or disconcerting experience. The goal of your conversation is to present *information*, not fear! Do your best to make sure that your good conversation doesn't provoke a sleepless night for any of you; thank you, Anne Morrow Lindbergh.

It is very helpful to consider, and plan out in advance, **What?** you want to convey to your Listener(s). You might even choose to script it.

SPEAK HONESTLY ABOUT YOUR HEALTH STATUS

When your health is good, it's incumbent upon you to tell your Listener(s) that. In fact—but only if it is true—the first and most useful information you can offer as you begin your communication, whether in person; in writing; or by telephone, Skype, or any other device, would be: "I am fine! My health is good, and I'm competent. That said, I do have some things on my mind that I'd like to talk with you about today."

After this preliminary introduction, you might then go on to explain to your Listener(s) that you've chosen to have a conversation with them at this point *because* you're well. *You may even want to mention your age (which can frequently serve as leverage to get and hold your Listener's attention, regardless of whether you think of yourself as young or as old).* Here's one hypothetical example:

> You know, it's nearly twenty years now since that bout of prostate cancer I had, and I'm thrilled to say that I'm still virile at seventy, and feeling great. I'm not going to name names, but three of my closest friends admit that they envy me! And not just because work continues to agree with me, although it does, as you know.

It may seem perfectly obvious to you, but be sure to say that having this conversation is really important to you. You appreciate them joining you in it, and mention that "it's probably a good idea for you to make some notes as we go along."

IN THE CASE OF ILLNESS IN THE INITIATOR

Not every Initiator will be able to honestly claim good health when beginning this conversation. It's far better to speak openly and honestly about your condition or any illness if and when that is the case. For instance, you might need to start by saying something like this about yourself, talking in a straightforward way:

> I'm as competent as I've ever been, but I have been surprised recently, after my annual physical, to learn from my doctor that my health may be somewhat compromised. I'd been putting off talking with you about some of the things we're looking into, but now I'd like to set a time to talk sooner, rather than later. Let's pick a time when we can get together, preferably this week, but within the month for sure. It's not that there's an emergency, but I'd like to tell you what I know about what's going on with my health, and to have your support.

Dad's Unexpected Illness, a Different Story

In one family I worked with, neither of their two adult, unmarried sons lived nearby. The dad, a venture capitalist who was considering retirement, was diagnosed with ALS, a neurodegenerative disease. When he was first diagnosed, he still looked and sounded like he always had. He and his wife decided to take advantage of this, and promptly asked "the children" to come down for a weekend. The parents had some things they wanted to talk about with their sons. Expecting a retirement discussion, the sons went along without hesitation with the plan to come down and talk the following week, rather than trying to postpone this conversation. Their parents, however, spent the week before the sons' visit going over their Last Will and Testament with lawyers and cataloging every piece of information about their closest friends and family members, health, finances, insurances, and so on. They put together virtually any information that they could think of that might become useful to these young men. They prepared lists of names, addresses, e-mail addresses, telephone numbers, passwords, and even time-zone differences.

Why were these parents so specific and detailed? It was clear to each of them that this news of Dad's very serious illness was going to be disorienting to their sons. Certainly, it had been and still was to each of them. By focusing on concrete details, the parents were both helping themselves sort out what needed to be faced and considered, and preparing to help their sons cope as well. While this doesn't mitigate shock, it does typically help Listeners to function in the face of unexpected and harsh news, as was the case for this family.

IT'S FINE TO ASK FOR A PROMISE IF YOU WANT ONE

It's perfectly reasonable for an Initiator to ask a Listener to make certain promises. The most pressing, primary questions people initiating this communication will want resolved are: "Can you promise to follow through with my wishes? Is that going to be possible for you?"

When Initiators introduce this question of willingness to follow through with their wishes early in their conversation, it's often hard for a Listener to immediately make the promise to comply. Listeners are apt to need to know more about what's wanted, what the Initiator's specific thoughts and wishes are, so they can assess what's being asked of them. Postponing the answer to "*Can you promise?*" is often hard for an Initiator to tolerate. Understandably, any Initiator wants a yes to be given immediately and willingly. But in truth, it's fair to all involved for a Listener to postpone making any promise until the question of what it is that's being asked of the Listener is more specifically explained and understood. The answer will often need to be held in abeyance for the time being, but hopefully without behaving like black coffee and depriving anyone of a good night's sleep.

The Listener's willingness and ability to promise affirmatively gets revisited at the end of the conversation, of course. By then, the Initiator will have communicated a great deal of factual information as well as his or her wishes

---

Working with a Script

Whatever the situation you find yourself in when you have this communication, consider having *scripted* your part of the discussion in advance so that you cover all the information you have in mind. You don't want nervousness to cause you to omit anything you consider important. The scripting could certainly be word for word, but it could just as well be brief, even in outline form, or with key words. The style of your script can be readily tested if you decide to do a dry run with friends, of course.

One further advantage of scripting your notes is that they can be readily e-mailed, scanned, faxed, messaged, or snail mailed to your Listener(s) after the conversation if you decide that would be useful.

---

about end-of-life care, and whether medical decisions will be shared responsibilities with a medical Listener or fall exclusively to this nonmedical Listener. Sometimes patiently waiting for an answer is very hard for an Initiator to do because, understandably, that person wants the yes to be given willingly and immediately. In truth, it's much better for the answer to be an honest one, based on knowledge, thought, and understanding, as well as, perhaps, love. Above all, if the ultimate answer cannot be a *yes*, perhaps the potential Listener can help the Initiator review other people whom they both know who would indeed be able to say yes, confirming a willingness to carry out the Initiator's end-of-life wishes as described. Alternatively, Initiators may have a backup choice of Listener and can put that choice into effect rather quickly and easily.

A STORY ABOUT GRANDPA LOUIE

I called my maternal grandfather "Grandpa Louie." I loved him totally. He was sweet, kind, funny, generous, and a successful man in the business of demolition. (He owned and ran a house-wrecking company.) By the end of his life, one of his three daughters and two wives had pre-deceased him. He continued to live in his original apartment with the one of his surviving daughters who was not yet married. My mother was his eldest surviving daughter, and she, my father, and I lived across the street from my Aunt Doris and Grandpa Louie.

Our families were close and often ate dinner together a couple of nights each week at our apartment. But I never heard any conversations about business details or Grandpa Louie's health, and certainly nothing about his finances. Talk was about commuting, pleasure trips, the news, the weather, when the circus was coming and how many tickets did we want, and what my aunt was doing. No one seemed to think any information was missing because, if they did, questions would have been raised by one of the grown-ups.

Beyond dinners, Grandpa Louie visited nearly daily after school and spoiled me, his only granddaughter. On each visit, he took me to the corner candy store, where we sat at the counter and had our egg creams and pretzels. We generally just had fun—usually laughing about silly things or reading comic books together. Some nights he stayed for dinner; more often he did not. His work days were erratic. He worked long and hard when there were jobs and less so when the jobs dried up.

My Aunt Doris was away on vacation when Grandpa Louie didn't visit or call for two days in a row. My mother became very concerned and on the second late afternoon, she went over to his apartment. She found him on the floor in his bedroom, near a radiator. He'd apparently fallen, hit his head, and had not been able to get up or even to crawl very far on his own. She called an ambulance and the needed medical help was immediate; he was hospitalized. Initially, Grandpa Louie was conscious, but not mobile. Our family visited him every day and, without ever being asked, my parents began to attend to his financial needs. When they looked for a checking account, to their utter surprise, they learned Louie kept all his assets in cash. His habit apparently was to make a ton of money and use it for family trips or to help out anyone who needed it; and he'd spend a good part of his money on rent, other bills, and gifts for the kids and grandkids, never worrying about debts being repaid to him. When times were tough, he trusted there'd be more good times coming. My mother and father in a sense became his *de facto* "Listeners" without Grandpa Louie ever actually *initiating* a conversation. They paid his bills, including those for the eight-week hospitalization with round-the-clock nurses, and when he quietly died after a heart attack during the night, they also took on the debt caused by his funeral and burial expenses. For a while, my folks were financially wiped out by doing all this. Even so, had they been asked if they would be sure to follow Grandpa Louie's end-of-life wishes, my parents would have had absolutely no hesitation. Their immediate, willing answer, as demonstrated by their actions despite the absence of directives of any kind, would have been, "Whatever's needed, whatever he wants, we'll do. We're family."

Contrast that with Caroline's experience.

Caroline's Story

Caroline had been born in Winnipeg, Canada, and moved south to Rochester, Minnesota, where her husband, Steven, was an obstetrician/gynecologist at the Mayo Clinic. They fell in love with Minnesota and became citizens of the United States and parents of three children, two boys and one girl. For years after the children finished college and began families of their own, Caroline and Steven worked, traveled, and generally enjoyed being empty nesters. They were in exceedingly good health, with the exception of Steven's occasional depression.

Steven and Caroline talked about the years to come and, when they were in their seventies, decided it was time to make a plan and be sure the kids would support it when the time came for their assistance. Expecting willing compliance, they set up a family meeting one weekend, but it turned into a fairly difficult situation for them. Because of religious disagreements, not a single one of their three children was willing to agree to their funeral and burial choices. There was a "united front" in opposition to their wishes. Not prepared for this, and not knowing what to do next, the couple abruptly ended the weekend's togetherness.

Steven slipped into a deepened depression at this time and refused medication or any other kind of medical help. Caroline was at her wit's end. This was not at all the outcome they had anticipated and they were unprepared with a next step.

Without any warning at all, Steven took his own life. Caroline was suddenly widowed, feeling isolated from her children, and personally very aware of Steven's wishes for his funeral and burial, as well as for the disposition of their estate. They had discussed all the details of these together, prior to their contentious conversation with the three children.

Caroline managed to do everything Steven had wanted. After things quieted down, however, she was faced with how to proceed to find a willing Listener for her own wishes. She was disconsolate.

One evening, unannounced, the daughter of a dear friend and neighbor literally came to her rescue. She visited Caroline within a month of Steven's death and asked if she could be of any help.

"I've talked with your kids, of course. They feel terrible, responsible perhaps," she related, "but they're still adamant about not being willing to comply with your 'unorthodox' burial wishes. Would you trust **me** to do that?"

Caroline wept in relief, surprise, and appreciation, accepting that offer without hesitation or need for further consideration.

EXERCISE: THE **WHAT?** OF YOUR CONVERSATION

Part 1—Factual Items

It's usually easiest to begin talking about factual, concrete topics in a conversation like this, so that's where I suggest you start your planning. While some items *are* pretty generic, in this exercise, I suggest you work with several categories so you can discover what you clearly want and need your Listener to know. This is a lot of work, so you may want to plan to devote a full day or more to each category until you've finished. The recommendations that follow are not intended as an entirely comprehensive list of items to include in the **What?** of your conversation. They are, rather, examples, and you will want to individualize your list according to your own needs and lifestyle.

Start with naming and organizing the *categories* you'll want your Listeners to know about. You'll begin to recognize the degree to which your Listener(s) will need to be involved on your behalf, and that, too, can be part of your conversation.

Some typical sample categories and their components follow. Of course, no one's needs are going to fit this picture entirely. You know yourself, your needs, and your wishes. They are the ones that are of paramount importance.

Generic

Included in this category are broad, relatively universal pertinent categories that Initiators will typically want their Listeners informed about, such as legal documents, business considerations, taxes, insurance, and real estate information and obligations. Each generic category includes factual information, not every category of which will be mentioned in this book. Rather, observing these broad brushstrokes of categories, each individual Initiator will become ready and able to cite his or her own generic areas of greatest importance. Many examples follow:

- If you have a safe deposit box, where is it? (List the bank's name, address, telephone number, and the name of any banker who knows and helps you at that branch.) Identify the additional signatories who have access to the box. Where do you keep the keys to the safe deposit box? Would you like your Listener to have one set of these keys, to keep things simple when it would be necessary to go to your box? If you do not have a safe deposit box, are you now thinking that having one might be a good idea? If so, go ahead and see if the most convenient bank can make one available to you, or keep trying until you find a bank that is able to do so.
- Who has power of attorney and where is that on file?
- Who has a durable power of attorney for health care, and where is that filed?
- Do you have, or can you provide, a compendium of all the information you use to access online data and accounts? Your Listener will need

to know, for example, what the passwords are for your computer, cell phone, tablet, access to the cloud, and all other similar information. Money can help you buy a replacement key to a safe deposit box if necessary, but almost nothing will help you get into computerized files when the passwords are missing! Be sure your Listener has the ability to access all of your electronic data.

- If you have young children, their guardianship, and so on, exemplifies things that you must attend to in your will. This book obviously mentions the topic, but offers no advice on the plans you might want to make. I do, however, encourage you to give this thought and make appropriate plans for the well-being of your children in the event you, their parent or parents, die while they are still minors. The well-being and care of a pet or pets may fall into this category as well. Your Listener should know what the plans are that you have created, where they are written and legally in place, and how to reach key people such as the designated guardian.

Financial

- Supply names, addresses, e-mail addresses, and telephone numbers for all people who have financial responsibilities for you: accountant, financial planner, office manager or bookkeeper, banker, and so on. Is your Listener known to each of these people, or are introductions in order, either by e-mail or in person? Set up any introductions that are needed.
- Social Security information is important for Listeners to know. For instance: What is your Social Security number? If you are already collecting your Social Security benefits, how much is your monthly benefit, and where and when do you receive that electronic (or paper) deposit?
- Do you have a Federal Employer Identification Number (EIN) for tax purposes? You will want your Listener to know what that designation is, and where and how you use it.
- Identify your primary assets and how they can be viewed. If you have an annuity, where would your Listener find it and all the details relevant to it? List all your assets, pensions, and other retirement plans, even estimating their current value if you can, and how to access each.
- Do you have insurance policies? (These go beyond annuities, possibly to include any of the following: medical and/or dental, life, auto, homeowners', renters', personal property, any umbrella policy, disability, long-term care, and so on.) Where will these be found if not in your safe deposit box? Be sure the beneficiaries on all policies are correct and up to date!

- Do you have a car or any other vehicles? Do you have car payments set up? If so, provide the outstanding loan amount, date payments are due, address payments are sent to, and how you pay these (i.e., online banking, check, or automatic payment).
- Do you pay a mortgage or rent? Once again, provide details on the amount, date due, address payment is sent to, and how you pay this (i.e., online banking, check, or automatic payment). Real estate deeds, documents including time shares, and all information related to these are helpful to organize and give to your Listener.
- Are there any other outstanding loans a Listener would need to know about?
- Review your check register to see which monthly bills you'd want the Listener to pay for you in the event of an illness, and make a list, including the above details for each.

Medical

- List your pertinent health history for your Listener, even if you think he or she is fully aware of it as a spouse, child, or best friend actually might be. Under stress, we all are subject to memory failures or just plain overlooking something. Concierge physicians today are supposed to provide a zip drive of some sort to their patients, updated annually after a full physical. If you have one of these, let your Listener know where it is and when it was last updated.
- List the name, area of specialization, address, telephone number, and e-mail information for each health-care specialist (this includes all MDs, dentists, therapists, DOs, chiropractors, etc.), as well as data about your pharmacy, physical trainer, and any other medical personnel with whom you are currently in contact at least once a year.
- List names of health insurance providers and types of plans you have. List telephone numbers and addresses for all policies, along with information on how you pay for them (bank online, check, or automatic payroll deductions). You may choose to discuss what to do about these policies if you become ill and need your Listener to have access to your accounts to pay your medical bills on your behalf. If you have minor children, provide the same information about their health insurance providers, if different from your own.
- List plans for organ donation, if applicable.
- If you have pets and you have not previously provided information about their veterinarians, health needs, and preferred kennel, include that data here under *Medical*.

Business or Professional

- If you are the principal of a small business, or its owner, are steps in place for your business to be able to continue without you? What are they?
- If no such steps are in place, how will your business end?
- Whether your business continues without you or closes, who will have to be notified, and in what way? Where is that information? Do you have an actual professional will or its equivalent? If so, make it immediately available to your Listener(s), or be sure they know where you keep patient, client, or customer information. This is necessary in case you are not retired at the time of your death, and there are people who work with you and will need to be informed in a timely manner. Don't count on the obituaries in the *New York Times* or any other newspaper to do this job for you!
- If you are involved in a small business, what, if any, are its rules of succession? What has been put in place for the business after the loss of mental capacity, debilitating illness, or death of the primary proprietor? Are you the proprietor? If so, this responsibility is fully your own!

While you are working with this suggested set of lists, you're likely to discover the names of documents that you don't have but now realize you need. There's time to make that happen. Contact the professional you think can help you and get started. For instance, if you realize you've never done anything about being an organ donor and want to, contact your lawyer, physician, or government office (e.g., the Department of Motor Vehicles) and ask for help setting that up. If you lack a succession plan for your small business, take the time to call either a colleague, your professional organization, or your attorney (or all three) and get the help you need to prepare that document to your satisfaction, as well.

In the case of certain types of professionals, including psychotherapists, it is becoming more conventional than in decades past to generate a Professional Will for your practice or small business. Members of the American Group Psychotherapy Association (AGPA) as well as Eastern Group Psychotherapy Society (EGPS), the American Association for Marriage and Family Therapy (AAMFT), and other professional organizations are sure to have members who have written and/or lectured about the creation of these ethical documents in addition to the planning and management of the professional's responsibilities regarding and during unplanned absence. There are many professionals who do work of this sort, and you may want to see what they charge and how long a process is involved while you consider if this could be useful for you and for your Listener(s).

We began this examination of **What?** so that you would be sure to tell your Listener about items that are mainly concrete and factual. For most people, generally speaking, these are the easiest topics to deal with. As you continue to plan what to tell your Listener, however, you're likely to find some materials that evoke intense emotions at times. My suggestion? Take a deep breath. See if it helps you to do some journaling. Keep working through this material, disquieting as it may be, however, either right then or at a specific later time that you think you will find more comfortable.

As we progress through planning **What?** to tell a Listener, we move gradually into the more emotional material that will be on an Initiator's mind as well. Here's an exercise that can be helpful for you when the emotional intensity ratchets up.

EXERCISE: THE **WHAT?** OF YOUR CONVERSATION

Part 2—Some Highly Charged Emotional Items

The items in this part of the exercise involve specifically personal decisions, primarily around end-of-life care. They may evoke any of a number of emotions. Once made, Initiator decisions may be subject to discussion, but not challenges, a fact you may want to emphasize during your conversation with a Listener.

When we look our own mortality in the face, it's the rare person who doesn't experience some level of anxiety or fear. This will be true both for Initiators and Listeners, by the way.

One of my teachers, Rabbi Zalman Schachter-Shalomi would emphasize how important it is to face our fear. He taught students of all ages and belief systems to discover how to live so that the fear would morph into compassion and even tenderness. Zalman was a proponent of "listening within" and hearing your own voice of wisdom. This process, he'd contend, was more valuable than being ruled by fears, including the fear of death.

Zalman took his beliefs a step further, teaching his students to "*live your life fully, and when the time comes, to let go.*" Pediatrician and psychoanalyst Donald Winnicott said something of the same. His words, or at least their sentiment, were "*I want to live until I die.*" Perhaps these simple but philosophical principles could be helpful to you, too.

Let's get back to planning your conversation. At this point, what you may feel ready to think about and then discuss is how you want to "let go and die peacefully" if you have the choice. How much do you want to fight to be alive, in case a time should come when that's really the question? Is there a point at which you want to stop fighting and just be made comfortable? In either case, what do you want your Listener(s) to know or to do?

- Have you had, or do you plan to have, a discussion of these matters with your doctor(s)?
- In case you are not able to express these wishes when the time comes, do you have a health-care proxy who is fully informed? If this person is not your Listener, the two need to be aware of one another, and their roles clarified.
- What are your wishes regarding life-support methods including (but not limited to) feeding tubes, a tracheotomy, and ventilators?
- What if you were to be in a vegetative state; what would you want your Listener(s) to do then?
- If you have decided that palliative care or hospice were the proper next step, would you want to be in hospice care in a hospital unit, in your own home, or in a hospice facility?
- What are your funeral and burial choices? If you want to leave these up to someone else, who is that person, do they know they will have this responsibility, and when is the best time to discuss that with your Listener(s)?
- If, like my parents, you've thought out what seems to you to make the most sense, when's the best time to bring this up and make your recommendation? Have you prepaid and/or prearranged for your funeral? If so, make sure your Listener has copies of all the agreements.

In the case of each of the above items, in fact, at every choice point in this book, be sure to mention the *rule outs* as well as your *wishes* as Initiators. One public figure I worked with in Connecticut was emphatic about a particular funeral home in which he did *not* want his body. "My body is none of their business!" he stated adamantly. "Someone has to be sure my children don't make that mistake!" I wondered if he was hoping I'd take on that responsibility, but I was able to convince him to add it to his list of things to clearly speak about to his adult children in order to be sure they knew his emphatic preference. When, eventually, he initiated a conversation with his children, he did include this information, and they understood and readily agreed to comply with his wishes.

EXERCISE: THE **WHAT?** OF YOUR CONVERSATION

Part 3–Some Very Hot, Emotion-Laden Family Issues

It seems to me that, by now, you are likely to have identified your wishes regarding the end of your life, in the event that you have time to prepare. If that's the case, then the next step for you is an assessment of any *family issues* that concern you. The real question here is: How would you like them to be handled in relationship to your end-of-life issues? If your religious or any other beliefs are such that they are at odds with those of members of your family, learn from the story of Caroline and Steven, and do your best to leave nothing to chance. Stipulate in writing what you want and who is responsible for making sure that happens.

For instance, suppose you are a Reform Jew and are choosing to be cremated; your cousin who's also your Listener has become a Conservative rabbi and does not approve of cremation. What happens to your body and your wish to be cremated? Now is the time to deal with any and all sticky issues of this sort, Jewish, Viking, Irish, and so on. Most heritages have issues of this sort that might present problems for a Listener if not clearly thought out, discussed, and put in writing while the Initiator is alive and sentient.

Now is also the time to plan ahead so that the people you hold dearest, who love you, will never have to sit in a hospital room with you, desperately wishing they knew what you'd want but no longer able to ask and expect you to answer them. You can prevent that if you're willing to—by thinking about it, and talking, writing, or otherwise clearly communicating your wishes to the people who love you.

A CASE OF LAST RESORT: BETH AND LARRY'S CONUNDRUMS

See if there's anything going on in this story that you identify with or can find useful for yourself. Larry's a psychotherapist and Beth has just recently retired from her very successful career as a marketing executive. Their life is happy together, empty nest and all, and they have very few problems. But they do have *one*, which, as they described it to me, "*is a doozy!*"

Larry and Beth are adults who are young enough to still have one set of living parents, Beth's, who are in their eighties. They live within thirty minutes of Beth and Larry, in an assisted living facility that had been wonderful for them initially.

Recently, Beth's dad's dementia worsened so much that he needed to be moved into what is called "Level 4 care." Her mom is distressed by this change and unhappy to be living alone in their original apartment. She visits Dad every day, spending nearly the whole day with him despite the fact that he doesn't know her or even that he's got a visitor. What makes this worse is that Beth and Larry recognize that Mom has no idea what Dad's end-of-life wishes would have been had they discussed them while he was still perceptive. She's become increasingly despondent, and the younger couple came to me, asking for some direction.

I immediately recommended that they set up a time for a serious conversation with Mom about her own end-of-life matters.

"What good will that do? She's not the demented one, nor is she in immediate need to put those wishes into effect," Beth said quickly, obviously dissatisfied with my suggestion.

"I understand that," I explained, "but if you find out what Mom wants for herself, and she does similar things for Dad who no longer can tell her or anyone else what he wants, it is likely Mom will be okay acting on these same decisions on behalf of her husband when they're needed."

"This is a sort of 'last resort' solution, then?" Larry intoned.

"Oh, I get it," said Beth.

A LISTENER'S TIME TO TALK

Listeners are apt to be filled with questions before you've finished telling them everything you've given thought to. There's generally a lot of information to go over. They might welcome an opportunity to express thoughts and/ or questions of their own at about this point. If you have the energy, and if the conversation has been face-to-face, now's a good time to take a coffee or tea break and regroup, listening to their comments. This might also be a propitious time to return to the subject of trust, what I think of as "the willingness question": *Can you promise to follow through with my wishes? Is that going to be possible for you?"* With all the facts and wishes out in the open, are you talking

---

A Caveat

We know that this is emotionally charged material that you're talking about, and too often, it's easy to forget or confuse material of this nature. It's a really useful idea for an Initiator to be talking from an outline and for the Listener(s) to be making notes as the conversation proceeds. You might even consider running through these notes together, to verify what's been said and to make sure nothing that's really important to you has been overlooked.

with a person who actually will be able and willing to follow through on your behalf, if or when it becomes necessary?

EXERCISE: PREPARE YOURSELF FOR
THE CONTENTS OF YOUR CONVERSATION

In this fifteen-minute writing exercise, you'll be having a conversation with yourself. I encourage you to think about and then write down some thoughts about the following four main questions:

1. What was it like for you to begin to organize your documents to make it possible for someone else, your Listener, to be able to access and perhaps attend to them?
2. When you finish this, will you feel ready to plan what to say when you have your actual conversation?
3. What more do you need in order to more fully be ready?
4. Do you need to create a deadline for yourself to encourage getting this information in order promptly?
    a. Is anything missing or stopping you from going forward? If so, write about it.
    b. Consider how you will include that material—those thoughts about what's missing for you—in your conversation. Next, make some notes so that you will now *be able to move forward* in effectively planning your conversation.

In groups, people often talk together, comparing experiences and feelings as well as raising some of the questions the work is prompting. One of the questions that seems always to be raised is "What is a Legacy Document and do I need one?" Perhaps that was on your mind, too.

A Legacy Document is absolutely optional. In my groups, we set up a separate time to talk about Legacy Documents. In the case of this book, Legacy Documents will be discussed in some detail in chapters 8 and 9.

FINGERPRINTS: THE STORY OF ONE
HUSBAND AND WIFE'S **WHAT?** ISSUES

Every person's life story is unique, but situations can often be similar. Sometimes we can even learn from situations that are not very much like our own at all. See if the story that follows has any value for *your own* planning.

This is the story of a husband and wife, Lou and Sandy, who agreed that they needed to work out their conversations separately with their children from previous marriages. Lou was divorced, and Sandy had been widowed. They each had two (now adult) children from their previous marriage. This second marriage was already twelve years old, without further offspring, and the couple had learned how to blend the families as best they could without "planning to compete with the Brady Bunch," as they put it. Choosing the Listener of both conversations was surprisingly easy; they each decided to talk with both of their children without their current spouse participating or even being present. But they *were* challenged by the question of **What?**. What exactly did they want to say? This was the perplexing part for them.

Their styles were vastly different, and the habits they'd developed for organizing their paperwork reflected that. Lou had been retired for several years when they attended a communication workshop I led. He had grown careless, keeping stacks of newspapers as well as odd documents all mixed together on a bed in the rarely used guest bedroom. He attended to his mail "when he got around to it."

Sandy, on the other hand, was a financial planner with a comfortably small business of her own. She insisted that their financial lives be kept separate—for her sanity. This also prevented major arguments, they acknowledged, laughing.

What Lou and Sandy decided to include in their conversations could hardly have been more different. He remained haphazard, and she acutely organized. No surprise! Listening to these two people plan, what I was reminded of, and want to be sure you recognize as well, is that *the most important thing about a conversation is that it reflect the style, thoughts, values, and needs of the Initiator.* While the Listener often looks back on it as a *gift*, the conversation's primary intention is to serve the needs of the Initiator. For this couple, that meant two significantly divergent sets of needs, which, with thought and advance planning, were successfully met in their two very different meetings. "Like fingerprints," they commented, "no two conversations are identical, even when they're about the very same topic."

WHAT? WILL LEAD US TO **WHY?**

The stimulation of a good conversation, particularly one with as challenging a topic as end-of-life matters, is different for each person. In chapter 5 we have worked on exercises to help us each (as Initiator) determine rather concretely **What?** information we want to convey to our Listener(s) about our end-of-life matters. Many of us have chosen to begin to outline the content of the end-of-life conversation that we've considered so far. In chapter 6, our focus will be a bit more philosophical, as we consider **Why?** we're so intent upon initiating a conversation about these end-of-life matters. For me, that was the easiest part. I knew firsthand the benefits of having known my parents' wishes, and I wanted to be sure that I made it similarly easy for my daughters. This is a tradition now, in my family. Its value is beyond words (although that's not saying it's easy).

6

Ask Yourself, Why?

That which we are capable of feeling, we are capable of saying.

—Miguel de Cervantes, Spanish Novelist (1547–1616)

*W*hy is it necessary for you to have this conversation about end-of-life matters? The goal of an end-of-life conversation is *communication*. As Initiators, we decide there is value to putting "on the table" information previously felt or thought about, but not discussed. When you talk about your end-of-life data and wishes in this context, you break taboos—a very positive step to take, which can also feel very difficult. (I know this firsthand. I've been both Listener and then Initiator for one of these conversations.)

As Initiator of an end-of-life conversation, you need to speak clearly and openly about your end-of-life thoughts and feelings. While this can seem very hard to do, it is something each person is, honestly, capable of doing. This is true whether you are at any kind of a transitional stage of life, become ill or otherwise incapacitated, or simply move from good health to gentle and gradual aging sometime before your death. Be sure that details of your wishes and feelings, which are very clear to you, are made equally clear to your Listener. For instance, if you would want something out of the ordinary, like a Viking funeral or interment, be sure to discuss at length what that is like and where to find the important details. Take nothing for granted, including that your Listener will remember Grandpa's Viking funeral and know exactly what you have in mind for your own!

Where you are in your life when you realize that you want to have this conversation about your own end-of-life matters is less important than the fact that you've been able to make the decision and take the first steps in planning and initiating your conversation. Clearly articulate the end-of-life matters you'd previously not considered particularly important to organize and talk about. This may include thoughts about your bucket list, as well as possibly a mention of some actual items on it. Reference to a bucket list may both inject some lightness into this otherwise dense topic and be provocative for the Listener as well as the Initiator.

There are many times in life that can stimulate these conversations. People commonly think about having an end-of-life conversation when they are aging and/or ill and want to put in order everything they can. This might arise in conjunction with a new or revised Last Will and Testament (written usually with the help of a trust and estate attorney). Are there other times that come to mind for you?

You might think about your end-of-life matters when you are venturing into parenthood, just before a first child comes into the family (either by adoption or pregnancy). The new parent or parents frequently consider many "what if" situations, and this includes: *"What if something medically unusual happens to me/us? What would I/we want someone (a friend, family member) to do?"*

In that context, I'm reminded of a couple I worked with many years ago whose "what ifs" were never discussed in advance but turned out to be dramatically more than hypothetical. James and Sue were in their twenties, excited about having their first baby, and entirely unprepared for the anomalous situation that followed. The pregnancy was uncomplicated, and the delivery began to follow an ordinary pattern as well. Suddenly, about fifteen hours into labor, problems began to occur. The totally unexpected outcome was a healthy child but one who was delivered from a comatose mother in a vegetative state. James, the husband and brand-new father, was distraught. What was the right thing for him to do now?

"If only I knew what Sue would want me to do," he lamented.

Many of their friends were also having first babies, and these couples were emotionally affected by this very sad, scary, atypical situation. They almost all began to think and talk about ". . . if I were in that situation, what would I want?" As the women attempted to figure out the answer, they went on to talk about their wishes in small groups and larger ones. They were making sure that spouses and family members knew and promised to abide by the wishes they were discovering they had in case of unforeseen circumstances, statistically unlikely though it was that a situation like Sue and James' would recur in their friendship group.

In most pregnancies, the outcome is happy and healthy for all involved, but even in the smoothest situations, new parents often face the realities of "suddenly" becoming responsible for a baby as well as for themselves and one another. "What if . . . ?" can become a topic of conversation—or avoidance. When it's spoken aloud, the conversation is often brief and almost casual.

It's another opportunity for relatively young adults to consider their end-of-life thoughts and wishes and to share them with an appropriate person. Servicemen and their families are all too familiar with this problem. Once the talking's been done, however, most people find they are better able to stop worrying about this "what if . . . ?" because it's no longer vague and shadowy.

Another brief story: Leslie was pregnant for the second time, and she was having persistent negative premonitions about the outcome of her pregnancy. Her mom's labor had been long and difficult, ending in a C-section, and the obstetrician had advised her mom not to attempt another pregnancy. "It's better to have one mother and one child," she'd been told, "than either one without the other." Leslie's first pregnancy had been textbook easy, and yet, she carried the shadow of that statement to her mom into her own second pregnancy. She urgently wanted her obstetrician to know that she wanted to survive the pregnancy, healthy, no matter what. She felt selfish about this and was uncomfortable telling her wishes to her husband. The compromise she worked out was to initiate a talk with her doctor and make her wishes—as well as her conflict—known. Leslie's trust in her obstetrician was well placed; happily, her life was never in question during the delivery. Perhaps most surprising was her realization that she had been able to let go of her fears as soon as she set up the appointment for that prenatal conversation about her wishes. Leslie listened to her own inner voice (of wisdom) and acted accordingly, and it served her very well.

Why else might a person consider having an end-of-life conversation? Healthy, happily married or partnered couples often recognize and celebrate anniversaries, especially at the ten-, twenty-, and thirty-year points. These people, most often ranging in age from roughly thirty to their fifties, are pretty much in the prime of life and enjoying themselves, despite their many responsibilities and challenges. As couples plan the celebration of an anniversary, it's not at all unusual for them to think about the future and identify both the good and not-so-good things that they may have to face. The "good" things are easy to consider. The "less good" might include difficult transitions or changes: for instance, how to live after your nest empties or career shifts, or your parents' lives evolve and they are aging rapidly or dramatically. Facing either the *good* or the *less good* category is apt to prompt thoughts of your own mortality and what you would want, probably way down the road, when the time comes to think about your own death.

As a family therapist, I often encourage couples to renew their vows privately, with one another, on some regular (could be annual) basis. I suggest that they think about things like: "What am I feeling this year about our relationship, and where do I want to consider making changes?" "Are we in a transitional stage of our marriage, and where do we go from here?" When a couple sits down to think about "What would I like to do differently?" they have an opportunity to include any thoughts about life-and-death decisions and their consequences. Here you have another appropriate time for initiating a conversation about your own end-of-life thoughts.

People of almost any age might also be stimulated to think and have a conversation about end-of-life matters when prompted by religious holidays, particularly around the season of Christmas and New Year's or at the Jewish holidays of Rosh Hashanah and Yom Kippur. *I know I certainly do!* At the time of each of these holidays, people of all ages seem more willing than usual to make resolutions or think about the future with a candor that is evoked by the season. As introspection occurs, either seasonally induced or due to life's stages, you may also discover opportune times to privately consider **What?** your end-of-life matters are, and **How?**, **Where?**, **Why?**, and **When?** to make them known appropriately to the right someone else.

Psychologist Abraham Maslow contended that a person, of any age, is consistently in a state of "becoming." No person is ever psychologically immobile; change or growth is a constant possibility. Motivated, either consciously or unconsciously, to find meaning in life, virtually every person spends some time thinking about the life he or she is living. *Those of us who journal do this often, even once or twice on some days!* Some people then *talk* about their thoughts, while others might write or express their thoughts musically or graphically, and so forth, as they mature (or simply as they age). These thoughts might even generate a conversation. "*Why,*" you are asking yourself, "*why would I have this conversation?*" One reason is that, time and again, we recognize that a Listener's life, as well as an Initiator's, is made easier once there's been a satisfactory communication. Apart from the re-sponsibility of remembering and carrying out the wishes expressed, *a Listener will be freed from having to wonder what to do when "that time comes."* In turn, Initiators of any age report that having end-of-life conversations, and perhaps preparing a personal Legacy Document as well (discussed in chapters 8 and 9) can be desirable and useful as some people choose to look at, evaluate, and attempt to picture what their wishes will be concerning the end of their life.

This is important enough for me to repeat. *Having a carefully thought-out conversation with a person you trust provides an opportunity for you, the Initiator, to put your mind at ease; and in turn and in the future, there is no second-guessing required on the part of your Listener(s).* Once you have made the opportunity to initiate a conversation and have communicated your thoughts and the rel-evant concrete information clearly, you can be confident that when the time actually comes for your life to end, the people you trust and love most, who respect you, will have already heard what you want and agreed to honor your wishes and will proceed accordingly, responsibly, despite their sorrow.

ESPECIALLY FOR PHYSICIANS

The requirement to "do no harm" is a major tenet of the ethical principles required of medical practitioners. With this in mind, physicians in disciplines ranging from internal and geriatric medicine to cardiology, oncology, hematology, neurology, and beyond are currently engaged in struggles relating to end-of-life conversations. In 2016, Medicare took the first steps to reimburse physicians for time spent in these conversations with their patients. Atul Gawande and Angelo E. Volandes, both physicians, have written outstanding books that focus on the need for and effects of end-of-life care conversations largely from the unique perspective of medical doctors. Even so, despite recognizing how important it is to have end-of-life conversations with their patients, physicians are having a very hard time initiating them. That's understandable both because we know physicians are human, and because this material is challenging for almost anyone.

My own experience provides me with a rather simple solution for physicians. *Go ahead and be vulnerable.* Your actual needs for communicating your own end-of-life wishes and pertinent details aren't really different from anyone else's. If you are willing to take the time and make the effort to initiate a conversation of your own, there are benefits that will also take effect for your patients.

Having been the Listener to my parents' conversation, and ultimately very appreciative of the experience, has prompted me (with a little prodding from my agent) to be Initiator of a conversation with my daughters about my personal end-of-life matters. These two experiences guide me as I teach and encourage others, physicians and laypeople alike, why and how to initiate conversations of their own. To those practicing physicians and other health-care providers reading this book, I urge you to think about, plan, and experience a conversation of your own. Your capacity for empathy toward your patients can only grow when you have experienced your own vulnerabilities in embarking on this experience. I expect that you'll use this knowledge to encourage the patients in your practice to initiate conversations of their own about their end-of-life wishes and concerns—with you, perhaps, as Listener of the medically relevant aspects.

A physician/patient end-of-life conversation will differ in some ways from those I generally refer to because it will be more specifically medical in content and will be more likely to happen when the patients are further along in their lives than many readers of this book may be. It is very likely that such a conversation will include advance directives. Nonetheless, the emotional experiences and the actual or imagined roadblocks will be comparable to conversations with nonmedical Listeners. *A health-care provider who has been an*

*Initiator or Listener will surely be a more expert and empathic guide for patients,
having first had the capacity to be human and vulnerable while doing his or her
own talking.*

Further, patients seem to be drawn to practitioners who have the sensitivity to have gone through the conversation experience. I encourage healthcare providers to resume reading this book *as participants*, recognizing that you have the added benefit and responsibility, as well as challenges, of being medically trained. This is not an experience in which most patients will find it acceptable to be told, "Do as I say, not as I do."

INITIATORS: BE SURE TO EXPLAIN WHY YOU'VE CHOSEN TO HAVE THIS CONVERSATION!

The person or people who are Listener(s) of your conversation will want, without a doubt, to know *why* you've chosen *now* to talk about these end-of-life issues and details. It's both wise and reassuring for you to talk honestly about **Why?** you've chosen to have a conversation at this particular time.

You might have decided to talk about end-of-life matters, aging, or death itself around a birthday. That's quick and easy to explain. Alternatively, it may be that you've read a book or an article that set you thinking; in that case, say so, and describe both the resource and your thoughts. If it *is* true, be sure to mention clearly that this is an ideal time to have this discussion because "I'm healthy right now and thinking quite clearly."

If that's not the case, it's important to start with an honest explanation of whatever information is appropriate. Earlier in the chapter you read about some of the reasons people initiate conversations. Here are a couple of others: If you've just met with your lawyer and drawn up a will, you might be prompted to do some talking, to initiate this conversation. If you've recently talked with a physician and have information about an illness, you might say, "There are some things about my health that I want you to be aware of, and now seems to me to be a good time for us to talk together." This, in fact, is what happened for Ethel and Robert, in the following rather unique story.

A Going-Away Party for Old Friends

Robert, eighty-two, and Ethel, his eighty-year-old wife of sixty years, found themselves in an unusual and very difficult situation. Both husband and wife had very recently received diagnoses that clearly meant their life expectancy, in each case, was quite limited. They each had a predicted *maximum* of four months left to live. They were rather atypical in their responses and quite courageous. To begin, within a week after their two doctor visits, they invited their children and adult grandchildren over to talk with them, and they *joked*.

As soon as everyone had arrived, grabbed a snack, and sat down in the family room, Robert began. "You know how the house looks just like it's always looked from the outside when you drive up to it? Well, we're about to make some radical changes on the inside!"

Ethel went on, "We've decided to renovate and redecorate the entire downstairs."

"Immediately," Robert added.

Their family looked puzzled and began to ask questions, which Dad silenced. An attorney, although retired for nearly twenty years from his long-term job as corporate counsel to a Fortune 100 company, he was organized. At this point, he distributed folders to each person present, and his wife pulled her own printed materials out from the table next to her chair. These papers included everything the couple thought "the kids" needed to know in order to take over and manage their parents' affairs when that became necessary, identifying who had power of attorney, who was to serve as the health-care decision maker, and so on.

"Renovation?" was a question that followed. Ethel explained.

"We have each gotten some surprising medical news this past week, and you need to know what we've learned, how we feel about it, and how we intend to proceed.

"Dad's heart is worn out, and he's clear that he doesn't want to endure any more emergency interventions, right?"

Robert nodded and went on, "And Mom's dizziness and loss of balance and memory, it turns out, are from a pernicious brain disorder that is going to cut her life short . . . fairly soon. . . . She has also decided that she wants to let this take its course and not fight it in any way except to be safe and as comfortable as possible."

Ethel added, "This is how we both want it! And so, we've decided to renovate and redecorate by changing the living room and dining room into two bedrooms, each with a hospital bed that we've already ordered, plus our two walkers, and now also two wheelchairs. We'll each have caretakers from hospice, around the clock, and we want you to know our plans and our wishes."

Robert chimed in, "We're planning a party at church, in a couple of weeks, too. For old friends and the whole family. Frankly, I'd like my friends to roast me while I'm still above ground and can laugh with them, rather than at my funeral. Mom wants to come to the party, but she's not looking to be roasted; that's not her style, as we all know!"

The "kids" were stunned at the news, but respectful, and in truth, these decisions weren't out of character for their parents.

The well-attended "going away" party, about a month later, was declared "a huge success." I was one of the old friends who attended, many of whom came from all over the United States, as did family. The roast was resoundingly funny, touching, and affirming of life, the food and drink delicious and plentiful.

The children who had been present for the actual conversation with their parents were able to minimize their feelings of shock and sadness as they talked with guests the day of the party, and *emphasized the comfort they felt from knowing what was happening to their family, plus what was needed and wanted by each of their parents,* as their illnesses progressed.

"These insights help us recognize and appreciate some of the reasons why communicating clearly and completely and talking together is so valuable," one said.

There is always great value to clear communication, whether in ordinary "I'm healthy and" situations or in one like Robert and Ethel's, instances in which health is compromised, and the end of a life is not far in the future. We find that the associated positive feelings during and after a conversation, flowing from comfortable and useful communication, pertains to Initiators as well as to Listeners.

The exercise that follows is always useful, but I think it is particularly relevant after reading Ethel and Robert's story. It encourages you to do something similar to what they did, which is to consider the friendships in your lifetime, the important relationships, and how you might want to treat these people as you review your life and consider your end-of-life needs and wishes. This is an exercise that will be productive at any time during your life, not only in the end stages.

Exercise: A Provocative Communication

Spend the next ten minutes thinking back over the good friends you've known but have now lost touch with. Make some journal notes with answers to these questions as well as any random thoughts you have as you proceed:

1. Who are the friends you are thinking about?
2. How did it happen that you lost contact with one another?
3. Can you describe an outstanding story that involved both of you? (Or a favorite story about only one of you that relates to your friendship in some important way.)
4. Thinking of this memory, is there something you'd like to be able to *communicate* to this person?

5. If now is a good time to make contact, of course, do that, by letter, telephone, e-mail, text message, photograph, or whatever communication method feels appropriate for you.

If this isn't the right time to experiment with communication, hang on to these journal notes, enjoy the memory, and recognize that the seeds of communication don't just sprout up overnight. Communication requires that the seeds of thought be placed into the fertile soil of memory and imagination, watered with kindness and perhaps *good* humor and the desire for a positive outcome, and be given time to grow and even flourish. Not all seeds survive beyond one growing season. Gardeners learn the differences between, and the particular values of, annuals and perennials, for example. Communication, equally, depends upon timing, preparation, and patience, particularly when an intimate conversation is the goal. By the way, if an intimate conversation does not feel like your ultimate goal, rekindling these memories and going no further is another valid way to explore your feelings and move on with the preparations for your conversation.

WHY THIS CONVERSATION MATTERS—MARJORIE'S STORY

Marjorie's story depicts her long, happy marriage and amplifies for us the importance of sharing information and of end-of-life conversations. She shared this story with a mutual friend of ours when she heard about this book that I was writing, and thought it might interest me. (It did.)

"I was born in Manhattan and met Edward, the love of my life, a premed southern gentleman, Catholic like me, from South Carolina, while I was an undergraduate student at American University. We married as soon as I was graduated. Edward's medical career as a hand surgeon shaped our lives in Virginia.

"After our thirty-fifth wedding anniversary, some strange things began to happen to Edward. He experienced challenging allergic responses to things that had never bothered him before. His breathing was affected, and sometimes he would have rashes. With no clear pattern, his medical colleagues were unable to figure it out. No diagnosis and no relief. An undesirable combination.

"Ed thought that it would be a good idea for us to move to another climate, so when he suggested that we rent a house in Arizona for a month to see how we liked it, and to see how living there affected his allergies, of course, I agreed.

"Because we'd always been so entwined with one another and readily shared confidences, I initiated the question that was on my mind without any fanfare. I'd been wondering whether we'd find a new church we were comfortable in, to go to while we were in the Arizona rental, or just stick with the one we'd always attended for the weeks we were in Virginia. Church was an important part of our lives, and I didn't expect my pondering to come as a surprise to Edward.

"Edward seemed startled, or disconcerted, by the question, however, and asked if it would be okay if we postponed the discussion a day or two while he gave it some thought. I hadn't anticipated that it would require much thought, but agreed.

"Two days later, as we relaxed before dinner, Ed referenced my question, but his answer expanded it well beyond anything I had expected. His style of communication had always been direct and to the point; this was no exception. Basically, he told me the following:

- He didn't care if we attended church in Arizona. Whatever I wanted was what he wanted.
- If or when anything happened to him, he didn't want a wake.
- He wanted to be cremated.
- He wanted me to carry his ashes wherever I lived, even if I moved a lot.
- He wanted his practice to close and not be sold to anyone.
- He wanted the medical building he practiced in to be sold and the money invested through our investment advisor.
- He gave me a list of names, addresses, and telephone numbers of the other people he counted on, including an accountant, a banker, two attorneys, doctors, and his favorite priest.

"I was thunderstruck and very frightened. Of the two of us, I'm much more the one to talk about feelings and details. I questioned him—gently—as to whether anything was wrong that he hadn't told me about. Nothing, he responded emphatically. He had heard my question about church, and that led him to thinking about mortality. His. But he never once mentioned the word *death* when we spoke, even though medicine, and therefore life and death, comprised such a large part of his professional world and therefore, in a sense, our life.

"We went to bed several hours later without any unusual events and no further conversation about church or anything else that we'd discussed. He'd told me everything on his mind. I'd received the information attentively and respectfully, and as far as he was concerned, no further talking was needed.

"Ed had had a very minor allergic response to something unknown after dinner, but took an antihistamine, which was his usual protocol, and seemed to fall asleep easily. In the morning, I woke first. When I reached over to wake Ed, I realized his arm was too cool and he didn't appear to be breathing. When the medics arrived, they confirmed that he had died of a silent, major heart attack sometime during the night.

"The shock and grief were ghastly. I was in a terrible state. But then, as a few hours passed and neighbors and friends and his colleagues found out and began to come over, something wonderful dawned on me: I knew everything Edward wanted me to do. What a gift. What a RELIEF. No guesswork was going to be needed!

"I realized that as soon as I was able to stop crying, I could cope," Marjorie concluded.

Marjorie's story about her life with Edward, all the information he had suddenly decided to tell her (in *their* conversation), and the shock of his unexpected death brings us to the key point of relating their story. **Why?** would you want to have this conversation? Marjorie was able to recognize and talk about her sense of relief, even while stunned and newly grieving. She felt a surge of lasting relief because *she knew with certainty what Edward wanted her to do* after he had died. To Marjorie's credit, she honored all of his wishes. Knowing that, she lives with a sense of relief, peace, and confidence, even though she misses Edward daily. The gift of a conversation provides these feelings for virtually all Listeners, and that is one major reason **Why?** you might choose to initiate a conversation of this nature for yourself.

It is atypical for a conversation to be followed so immediately by a death, as happened with Edward and Marjorie. When an Initiator is in good health at the time of the conversation, it will usually be many months, years, or even decades before the imparted information needs to be used. In Marjorie and Edward's case, the conversation was followed immediately by his unanticipated death, which was stunning. And yet, despite her grief, Marjorie almost instantly sensed how their conversation had been an important gift to her. She had all the information she needed to take the steps Edward had wanted in case of his death. No guesswork was needed, and Marjorie, a grieving widow, could feel relief. This response is frequently experienced and described by Listeners; knowing this allows Initiators to be at peace as well.

The story of Ethel and Robert and their "going away" party further reflects the value to both the Initiators and their Listeners of talking together, openly and kindly. Too many Americans seem to prefer denial to thoughtfulness when thinking about their own death. For Americans, thinking and/or talking about one's death seems to be difficult at any age or stage. To a large extent, denial is the unspoken way of avoiding it. There's no question but that most people, most of the time, would prefer to be alive. There is, however, no cause and effect between preparing for and having a conversation about your end-of-life matters, and then dying. Edward's situation was entirely anomalous.

A conversation about end-of-life matters really doesn't take very long to initiate and complete. I encourage you to give it some thought, do the necessary talking, and then recognize that you're free to get on with living and enjoying your life, no matter how long or short a time remains *with a sense of well-being* as a result of the accomplishments that flow from a satisfying conversation.

A "LIFE-CHANGING" STORY

Jack, a psychotherapy colleague of mine, was present at a lecture I gave on the subject of my parents' unexpected conversation and its ramifications in my life at many stages. He was stunned by the story. It made him reconsider where he and his wife, Margot, were in their own preparations. They had created the necessary documents, a will and such, but upon hearing my remarks, Jack suddenly recognized how much there was that they had never considered doing, and he wanted to expand what he called their *"repertoire for end-of-life thoughts."*

He actually called Margot from his office between sessions that day and suggested they go out to dinner that evening to have a conversation without the need to cook and clean up. She thought that was a great idea and didn't even ask what it was he wanted them to talk about. They did indeed talk, and Jack repeated some of my family stories and how important he felt it was that they do more preparation than they had so far. Margot, a teacher, was intrigued at the prospect of giving thought to more than just the functional aspects, and she was quick to agree. Jack e-mailed me late that evening, asking for the outline of my lecture to use as a guide so they could develop their own conversations based on it.

Recently, I had dinner with Margot and Jack, and while it was over a year since my lecture and their active response, it was actually the first thing Margot mentioned when we sat down! *"Life changing"* is what they refer to it as. *"An expansion of what we had thought on our own was a good idea and already begun to carry out!"*

WHY? DO WE HAVE THIS CONVERSATION?

As Jack and Margot remarked, "How could we not?" Once you yourself are convinced that it's a conversation you want to have, more questions follow.

In chapter 7 we'll discuss two of these additional key questions, **How?** and **Where?**, both important to the task of conversation advance planning. I believe that it's helpful to both Initiators and Listeners for each of these aspects to be carefully thought through before the talking begins. My parents seemed to have made their decisions in haste, without much advance planning at all. However, I know I'll always remember that they spoke to me on the telephone, and recall visually how I changed extensions from one in the kitchen, then, after I quickly talked to my daughters, I walked into my office, picked up the second extension, and began making notes of the vast amount of information my parents were giving me. I imagine my folks on two separate extensions in the same room, their living room, while we spoke: my dad at his desk seated in his big desk armchair, my mother sitting comfortably on the couch. As you read chapter 7, with the questions **How?** and **Where?**, see where your imagination takes *you*.

7

Ask Yourself, How? and Where?

Life is not what it's supposed to be. It's what it is. The way you cope with it is what makes the difference.

—Virginia Satir, American Author and
Social Worker (1916–1988)

PART 1: **HOW?**

*Y*ou've already answered three of the key questions to help focus and develop our conversation:

- **Who** (will we talk with)?
- **What** (will we want to talk about)?
- **Why** (are we having this conversation at all)?

Part 1 of this chapter, which primarily focuses on the question **How?**, will also talk about communicating skillfully. Having read this far, and having given thought to the above three key questions, it's likely that you are reasonably confident that there's demonstrable value in thinking about, and then talking about, your own end-of-life matters. What's more, you've chosen carefully and are as sure as you can be that you will be able to trust the person or people you've selected to carry out your wishes, your Listener(s). You've asked, and they've assured you that they are able and willing to represent your wishes and act on them at the appropriate time, before, during, and after your death. In most cases, everyone can be very clear that they hope that event will be in the distant future! You've made a lot of progress, but you've still got more work to do as you prepare to really make this discussion happen.

How Will You Greet Your Listener(s) and Begin Your Discussion?

You will want to give serious thought in your own mind to the question **How?** and answer it to your personal satisfaction before you gear up for this discussion. I want to remind you of one point we observed back in chapter 3, when the woman initiating the conversation about a haircut started speaking with a complimentary, positive statement. This overture led to a useful answer, willingly given. There's not a thing wrong with telling your own Listener(s) something positive, like how much you love, appreciate, or respect them. You might start with how dear to you each person is . . . or a memory that comes from a long time ago. The start to your conversation is an important element as you attempt to discover **How?** to hold your conversation.

We'll spend some time in this chapter exploring successful communications, understanding what they are like, and what they may have in common. Our goal? To increase your own chances of having a successful conversation on this delicate topic of end-of-life matters.

Joe's Story

Joe was a single sixty-six-year-old man who had struggled through organizing his thoughts around the **Who?**, **What?**, and **Why?** of a discussion. He decided he would talk with Jenny, his youngest cousin, and Michael, her husband, both of whom he liked and respected. He felt certain they'd be willing, if not exactly happy, to join him in this "venture," as he referred to it. He was ready to send them an e-mail, inviting them to be his Listeners and then going straight into the details he'd been thinking about—the **What?** and **Why?** material. Joe had come to our group this week wanting approval for communicating the thoughts and wishes he was about to express by e-mail to his prospective Listeners.

Well, to Joe's surprise—and disappointment—not one member of this group approved of his tentative answer to our question, **How?** *"An e-mail?"* was the group's uniform, disapproving response. Sue, one of his friends in the group, questioned him very directly, looking him straight in the eyes as she asked in a quiet, nonthreatening tone, "How scared are you, Joe?"

In a later discussion, Sue admitted that she felt she was taking a chance asking this question this way, but she was also sure that catching him off guard would be the best (maybe the only) way to get an honest answer to her question. She wanted to find out the truth of what was going on for Joe.

Taking a deep breath, Joe slowly and candidly admitted, ". . . *very*." And then, "Yeah, I'm very nervous! I don't wanna get turned down. . . . I want them to say yes to me."

In a flash, this group went into action. Joe clearly was not the only one who'd become anxious doing the homework for the question **How?**, several other group members admitted.

Optional Exercise: Reduce Your Anxiety

1. You might be feeling some anxiety about the question **How?** yourself. If you're aware of any anxiety on this topic, go ahead and make some notes about it in your journal.

2. Sometimes, just acknowledging a difficult feeling is enough to "quiet it down." If so, go back to your journal and write a bit, admitting to the difficult feelings and your desire to release them. Alternatively, you can do your best to remember and picture a time in your life before now when you felt this level of anxiety. When was that? How did you manage those anxious feelings at the time? Can you use that same method to help release your anxiety now?

3. If you feel without resources for managing this anxiety, let me suggest some basic stress release or reduction methods:
   - Take ten deep inhalations to the count of four, and ten slow exhalations to the count of six.
   - Take a run or race walk (indoors or out) for ten to twenty minutes.
   - Do some relaxing yoga stretches.
   - Take the time to write some more about your anxiety in your journal.

The anxiety provoked by addressing and attempting to answer this question **How?** seemed to all of us in the group to come from dearly wanting Listeners to understand and immediately go along with all of the Initiator's goals, or directives. But reality was hard to overlook. It was possible that it would not be so easy to have it work the way the Initiator was proposing. At least initially, your wishes might have been rebuked, or perhaps only questioned, but neither of those responses is what an Initiator wants as the immediate outcome. You want to have your Listener continue nodding *yes*, all through this discussion. You want your thoughts and wishes to be agreed to right away. Assent is your goal, not dissention, disapproval, or disagreement. Sometimes an Initiator has to be patient and wait for Listeners to absorb the information, give it thought, and then respond honestly to their willingness to be a Listener . . . either yes or no.

Let's return to the group with Joe and Sue as participants. Just as we were turning our attention to another exercise, Joe spoke out, looking directly at Sue. "I'm doing this, staring at you, on purpose, Sue. You taught me something when you asked how scared I was. I don't know if you did it on purpose or by accident."

"What are you talking about?" Sue interrupted, sounding afraid she'd done something wrong.

"Well, even if it was just automatic for you, it was still great for me! Sue, look at me, please!" She did.

"When you spoke to me, you closed the potential distance between us. . . . You looked me right in the eyes, verbally asking your question but looking at me at the same time. I felt you caring about me, with that eye contact. It was a great help to me. I kind of knew it was okay to be honest. That can never happen if I stick with wanting to do this by e-mail."

In this particular group discussion, it became clear just how important—and sensitive—an issue the **How?** of these discussions can be. The following exercises were part of the group homework, guiding their work—and now yours—with the preparatory key question **How?**.

Exercise: Getting to *How?*

Part A   Give yourself five minutes, during which you'll come up with a viable picture of exactly **How?** you would be comfortable setting up your plan for talking. Have available nearby any notes you may need as reminders of your own decisions about **Who?**, **What?**, and **Why?**. Your mental image of **How?** may require two parts:

1. Pick a method of communicating your invitation to talk together. You can choose to do this either by telephone, e-mail, snail mail, Skype, or face-to-face contact. . . . It's your invitation. Add any other options that you find possible and appealing.
2. Once you've selected the method you prefer, flesh out the steps you'll be taking to get the outcome you prefer, and write them down. For instance, if face-to-face is your first choice, **how** will you cause that to happen? Will you leave a telephone message? What would you say?

Think through the details for whichever way you'd like to proceed, and by all means, feel free to make notes for yourself.

Part B   Allow a flexible ten minutes for this part of the exercise.

1. You've chosen a method, so you've thought through its pros. Jot them down, and add any new thoughts of advantages that come up.
2. Next, become your own devil's advocate. See what obstacles or deterrents to your choice come to mind. Keep track of these, as well.

On balance, do you still like your original method? Or do you want to change it? Go ahead and make any changes you think will be better for you, that is, that will help you move this discussion forward into really happening and being successful for you.

Let's Get Back to Joe

Joe had done his homework exercises and had chosen, in his initial e-mail, to combine his invitation to participate in this discussion (so important to him, about his thoughts and wishes for the end of his life) and meaningful pertinent details. Members of his group felt that he'd be making a mistake to do that and told him so. Joe was surprised but also appreciative of the caring and honesty he experienced, even as people disagreed with his initial plan.

Ultimately, Joe decided to divide his approach. He e-mailed Jen and Michael, asking them to join him for brunch on a Sunday later that month. He noted that he was fine and hoped they were, too. He had some things he was hoping to discuss with them, however. He'd grown aware that he "isn't getting any younger" and wanted to talk with them in person if they'd be willing.

Joe's group liked this approach, and several adopted it themselves. Of particular value was the mention of his good health. Remembering my own anxious response to my parents' unexpected telephone call, and my worry about their well-being for months afterward, I know that putting the Initiator's good health right out there, front and center, is a very helpful practice. As I've noted, it is equally valuable to be honest with Listeners if good health is no longer the Initiator's condition. The key here is honesty. Listeners have the right, indeed the need, to know what's actually going on for and with the Initiator.

Initiator Choices

Back to the choices you will be making as an Initiator and how you will be introducing them to your chosen Listener(s): When you've made a decision that feels right to you, it's often a useful idea to outline it, or even elaborately develop a word-for-word script for yourself. This is especially true when the method you've chosen is a telephone call, and the notes won't be visible to anyone but you, the Initiator. If you're going to be face-to-face with your Listener(s) when the discussion takes place, a full script is probably not a good idea, but outlined notes can be very handy. You want to help yourself remember everything you intend to say and to make sure you stay on track as your discussion progresses. How can you most effectively do that for yourself? For many people, notes turn out to be the best method. See if you can come up with any alternative methods that you like better.

*It's Time to Choose Your Method of **How?***

As so often happens in groups and workshops, initially it seems as though everyone has a different opinion and a different personal choice about **How?** he or she would proceed. That's not a problem! Conformity is absolutely not a requirement.

There are numerous **How?** choices to consider. From my personal experience, I'd suggest not going through your actual conversation points via e-mail, although you might take a chance and e-mail your invitation to talk together. The big complaint that we almost all recognize about e-mail is that it isn't a medium that allows for nuances. The subject matter, your end-of-life thoughts and wishes, is sensitive enough. I do not recommend potentially creating additional burdens on your communication.

For some people, handwritten letters might be the instrument of choice for this discussion of end-of-life matters. There are circumstances in which an individual, personal, handwritten letter is a desirable way to communicate, either for the invitation or in the conversation itself. If you have only one Listener, a handwritten note or letter might be both easy and a good idea, but if you have two or three or more Listeners, it's a method that becomes cumbersome. If, however, it remains your preference even when there will be multiple Listeners receiving your handwritten letter, be sure to let the recipients know that they are part of a group, as well as who the other members are.

My Aunt Irene was widowed, had no children, lived in Florida, and had many nieces and nephews with whom she always wanted to communicate as she aged. Irene was old in the days before computers, and she was too arthritic to bother with her Remington manual typewriter. She chose to handwrite the same page-and-a-half letter to all six of us. (We checked, believe me, to make sure our letters were identical.) In the twenty-first century, it's substantially less likely that someone would choose to send multiple, identical handwritten letters, but if that's your preferred method, go right ahead with it.

How Will I Be Able to Recognize a Successful Communication?

As we lay out the groundwork for a communication (whether a conversation or a letter of any kind), I'd like to include this criteria for evaluation because I think it is important to apply. The question is: *How will I know if my communication "worked out well"* . . . *if it was successful?*

A Successful though Not Perfect Conversation You Know About

Think back for a moment to my story in chapter 1 about my parents' taboo-breaking telephone call. I, the Listener, had had no warning before the

Exercise: Evaluating Success

While each person must make an assessment of his or her conversation individually, I suggest that you consider applying the following four criteria to determine success. Ask yourself these questions:

1. Are you satisfied that each element of your wishes has been identified and discussed as needed, either from your notes or your excellent memory? (Frankly, I prefer to use notes if I'm working under any sort of stress, rather than to tax my memory unnecessarily.)
2. Can your Listener(s) express (to your satisfaction) an accurate understanding of what your wishes are (by repeating them to you)?
3. Are you confident that your Listener(s) will be able, specifically and clearly, to express willingness to carry out your stated wishes?
4. Are you and your Listener(s) each capable of moving on with the primary task of living your lives well, without anxiety about what choices will need to be made, for you the Initiator, at the actual end of your life? This means that the responsibility the Listener has taken on is not one that will hamper his or her ability to move forward in life without undue anxieties, and the same will be true for the Initiator when the communication has achieved its goals.

If you honestly can answer "Yes" to each of these four questions, then you can trust that you and your Listener(s) have succeeded in experiencing a successful communication.

conversation began, either about when or what would be involved. This admittedly caused me anxiety when we finally started talking, and I learned, suddenly, what this conversation was about. Even so, both my parents and I would have considered our conversation successful in light of the four criteria in the text box. My parents had described what they wanted fully and with sufficient clarity that I understood what was being asked of me, and they knew that I was willing to comply. Once that was agreed upon, we each went about living our lives in an ordinary fashion until the moment came, eight years later, for me to remember and carry out my mother's wishes.

A Segue to **Where?**

Conveniently, we're going to consider other options concerning **How?** you carry out the discussion of your end-of-life matters with your Listener(s). Listen for the **Where?** information, as well. It follows.

Some people successfully ask Listener candidates to meet them for lunch, brunch, dinner, tea, or coffee . . . either in their home or at a restaurant. (Do you see that **How?** is linked to the beginning of an answer to **Where?** As in, *where is it okay to hold our conversation?*)

Public places or private ones are all possibilities. So are venues new to you and/or your Listener or those that all or any of you have gone to previously. One key factor: whenever it is possible, the Initiator hosts, wherever the meeting is scheduled.

PART 2: **WHERE?**

We're watching the natural evolution from the **How?** of your conversation to its next logical question, **Where?**. Once the invitation to talk together has been sent out and accepted, all the pieces are in place. Or they are supposed to be.

Janet's Story

Janet had done what she fully expected was all the preliminary work she'd needed. A divorced, sixty-year-old elementary school teacher, she knew the Listener she'd be talking to was her son, Larry, her only child, who was thirty-four. She'd invited him for lunch on a school holiday "to talk," at a restaurant they both liked in the town where she lived. (This town had been Larry's childhood hometown.) A businessman, Larry's hours were pretty much his own, and he was happy to do as she requested.

In advance of their lunch, Janet had organized a folder for Larry containing all the details she wanted him to know about if he was willing to be her Listener. It also contained a key to her safe deposit box, a bank signature card to give him access to her box, and more. She'd outlined her thoughts, and knew she could refer to her outline if she was inclined to. Janet felt she was on the young side to be having this conversation, but the idea of doing it had energized her, and she was excited to be the first of her friends taking stock in this fashion and "*getting it out of the way*," as she referred to it. Her **Who?**, **What?**, **Why?**, **How?**, and **Where?** were all accounted for, thought through, and even her **When?** (at lunch, on a school holiday) was in place. She was ready!

When Janet got to the restaurant, she was disconcerted to find Larry sitting at a table for three with his wife, Susan. *What the . . . ?* was her immediate reactive thought. She was startled, unhappy, caught off guard, annoyed, and confused. But as she walked toward them, she realized that they were holding hands. That made her immediately wonder what it was that had caused this change (in her ever so carefully thought-through and organized plan).

She approached the table carefully, unsure of what was going on, and sensing that her own scenario was not likely to be carried out today. "Susan!" she began, "I wasn't expecting to see you today. Are you okay?" She kissed Susan first, Larry next, and then sat down herself. The "kids" were all smiles, so she asked, "What's going on?"

"Oh, Mom," Larry began, "we're pregnant!"

"Finally," Susan added.

"Whew!" Janet thought. "Now what do I do?" This was a contingency that no one in my groups had anticipated, and so I mention it here for you to think about yourself. It is possible that, despite all your planning for this conversation, when you are ready to have it, your Listener will have an entirely different agenda, either by chance or design. Grace under pressure? That is what was called for.

Janet did fine. To begin with, she was indeed healthy, and further, she was thrilled at the prospect of becoming a grandmother. She recognized that this wasn't going to be the day to give Larry the folder, but that it would be smart to reschedule with him fairly soon. She knew this was easily possible to do. Without a whole lot of acting required, she coped by moving into their anticipatory space of the pregnancy and got happily involved.

Let's hear it for Janet, and for being flexible!

How to Decide **Where?**

To a large extent, the choice of **Where?** also falls to the Initiator. This will be impacted by circumstances to some extent, for example, when the Listener(s) live at a distance, have infants or child care to worry about, or have workdays that are inflexible. With all that understood, it's still up to the Initiator to select a place all those involved in the conversation can get to, at a time that causes no one undo difficulties. Any convenient meal, either at the Initiator's home or a sufficiently quiet restaurant or a park, beach, or public space that affords some privacy might be viable answers to **Where?**.

Where Shall We Talk?

There's a bewildering array of alternatives to face when we get to answering the key question **Where?**. Initially it would seem to be easier than the earlier four questions we have worked on—and perhaps it is. Let's tackle it.

Exercise: Let's Sort the Choices

It's time to go back to your journal and open to a clean page. Divide the page in half vertically and head the left column with your own name and **Initiator**.

The right column takes the title **Listener(s)** and the name of your Listener(s). Now it's time to complete the items in the two lists.

1. What would be the places where you'd be comfortable having your communication? List them all in the Initiator column. When you've run out of options, number them in order of your preference.
2. Now take a minute or two to get some water or a snack, stretch, do whatever it takes to move you away from this stage of the exercise.
3. Return to your journal, and in the Listener(s) column, list all the places that you think would be acceptable and convenient for your Listener(s). Number these options in their preferred order to the best of your ability.

Take a look at your two lists. Do you have congruent choices for any venue at all? If so, that's your **Where?**. If not, you need to go back to the drawing board and rethink your options. See if you can modify any of your answers on either list. Can you think of alternative options?

If you truly are unable to find a choice of place that suits both Initiator and Listener, you'll need to ask your Listener(s) directly to join you in deciding on the best place for getting together. (You need to be willing to join in at whatever place is named, at this point. Being stubborn isn't helpful, and you, after all, are the one who cares most about having this communication take place!) Go ahead and be flexible; it'll work in your best interest.

I want to emphasize that reaching an impasse over the question **Where?** almost never happens! Initiators rather instinctively know where the meeting should take place. Whether to meet face-to-face or by telephone is apt to be the more difficult issue, and we've addressed that question already.

Doug, Susan, and Mom: A Story of Coping by Compromise

Mom had two unmarried adult children, Susan and Doug. They lived thirty or so miles apart from each other, and all three of them had demanding jobs. Mom had been divorced since the children were young, and she had reached her mid-fifties with the recognition that, occasionally, people her age died. Her sixty-year-old neighbor, a man in excellent health, had tripped while walking on the sidewalk, slammed his head on the pavement, and six weeks later was dead. This made her apprehensive, and she called me for an individual consultation.

Mom moved easily through all the talking points and the considerations and choices she had to make, and then got stuck on **Where?**. This was the question that caused her concern. Initially, it was perfectly obvious to her that "the kids" would meet her at her house after work on a Friday, and they'd talk as much as they needed to and then go out for dinner. She had it all planned, but when she called to invite Doug, she found out that he'd broken his ankle playing tennis the previous day. Except for not being very mobile, he was fine.

The venue had to change—to Doug's. That made Mom feel cranky! She wanted to be the loved, important family member while initiating this conversation, but maybe Doug was going to be the star. Should she wait until she could have her way about where they'd meet? What was the best possible choice?

Mom was stymied, and she hadn't even spoken to Susan yet. However, being analytically trained for her marketing work, she was able to assess the situation. She decided that having the conversation sooner was better than requiring that it be in her own home. She got back on the telephone, making a conference call to both kids this time, and set up Friday evening the following week. **Where?** At Doug's, of course, and then to their favorite restaurant, which was quite close to his apartment.

Where? rarely needs to get in the way of moving forward. Unless the distances are significant or someone lets ego cloud the communication, it's generally the most straightforward of the key questions to answer.

THINKING AHEAD TO LEGACY DOCUMENTS

Since we've now covered five of our six key questions, it seems logical that you'd wonder where we're heading next. We've been shaping our communication about our end-of-life matters and preparing to decide what we want to do about carrying it out. In groups that I've led or in my lectures and workshops, at some point during our discussion of issues surrounding this end-of-life conversation, inevitably questions came up about personal Legacy Documents. In the next two chapters, we're going to answer, to the best of my ability, many of the questions that I have been asked frequently about these Legacy Documents.

δ

Do You Think You Might Like to Write a Legacy Document?

On occasion, I like to reread my grandfather's letters. . . . While leafing through them, I'm saddened by what is being lost in modern communication.

—Kristina McMorris,
Living American Novelist (birthdate unavailable)

We're moving toward a conclusion in our discussion of breaking the taboos of silence and discovering how to talk effectively about end-of-life issues. There is still one more segment of work to consider relating to our key questions, and that is in chapter 12, where we address the sixth and final key question, **When?**. First, however, in chapters 8 and 9, we're going to focus on personal Legacy Documents—what they are, why you might want one, and how to write one—in the event that you want to create a Legacy Document of your own. Chapters 10 and 11 will look, respectively, at potential or actual obstacles to effectively communicating end-of-life matters and then at some of my personal reflections on the major topics in this book in general. This chapter begins by addressing some of the questions on the subject of Legacy Documents that have come to my attention in workshops or lectures.

There are many reasons you might choose to write a Legacy Document, and approaching or thinking about the end of your life (if you feel or fear that it is drawing near) is one possible catalyst, but it is by no means the only motivation. Rather, at some point in life, perhaps like Kristina McMorris's grandfather, you realize that if *you* don't preserve your thoughts and stories for the future, no one else can or will. Autobiographies or memoirs of many kinds are popularly written by people in all stages of life, often to create a personal Legacy Document, either consciously or unconsciously. We each actually do have something to describe, in writing, through video or audio,

Legacy Document or Ethical Will?

The confusion surrounding the differences between Legacy Documents and Ethical Wills probably derives from the fact that they have many similarities:

- You learn a great deal about yourself when you embark on preparing either document.
- Each is valuable.
- *Neither is a legal document.*
- In the case of each of these categories of document, an Initiator is hoping, or intending, to impart to future Listeners some of the knowledge derived from his or her life experiences.

As we age, most of us manage to learn. What we learn has meaning to us, and we frequently want to share that meaning with future generations, that is, to an expanded audience of our identified Listeners. Both Legacy Documents and Ethical Wills provide methods for that sharing. In twenty-first-century America, these documents can readily be created by anyone who chooses to make the effort. They are prepared by people of all faith traditions, ethnic backgrounds, ages, income brackets, genders, and levels of education.

In casual usage, the two terms are thought by many people to be synonymous. They are used interchangeably in many instances, and the distinctions blur. It's hard to deny that, in some instances, Legacy Documents and Ethical Wills mean almost the same thing since each allows for a sharing of experience with future Listeners. *But technically they are not identical.* Although a distinction may often be considered unnecessary and only a matter of the speaker's or writer's preference, in fact and by definition, Legacy Documents and Ethical Wills do differ.

The word *legacy* speaks of something handed down, usually understood to mean something handed down from the past, *some form of inheritance, most often of value.* A Legacy Document is a document of any form that contains information about values that are being handed down as an informal type of inheritance, usually transmitted through stories. For the purposes of this book, a personal Legacy Document supplements the Initiator's communication with the identified Listener(s) of choice, and it may also expand that communication field, as we will see. *A Legacy Document is a personal document, not a legal one.*

An Ethical Will goes beyond "story" to typically emphasize right and wrong conduct options and preferences, affirming particular principles of relevant ethics and morality. Historically, Ethical Wills were exclusively verbal in form, virtually always issued by men, as seen initially in the early days of Judeo-Christian cultures. In biblical and also medieval times, Ethical Wills were generally recognized as binding. Like its sibling, the Legacy Document, however, *an Ethical Will is not a legal document!*

As our societies moved into modern times, written records of these documents appeared, and the newer phrase, Legacy Document, has become popular. There are people who contend that these two kinds of documents are very different from one another, and those who counter that they do the same job and are therefore the same. I see subtle differences based on the definitions of the key words, *ethical* and *legacy*, and I have chosen to use the more contemporary phrase, Legacy Document, throughout *Your End of Life Matters.*

or graphically, that could be of interest and value for future generations. The transmission of any of these parts of what we learn to think of as our legacy is where a Legacy Document plays a valuable role. The role itself has many possible styles or forms.

For example, the Declaration of Independence is used as a Legacy Document for one branch of my family. They have always gotten together for the Fourth of July. That is their "real" family holiday, much more important to them than Thanksgiving or Christmas or any of the other typically popular family occasions. Their Fourth of July celebration was actually very much a part of their *mother's legacy* to her sons. The family always knew—because Mom made no secret of this—that to her, the Declaration of Independence was the most important legal and ethical document there was. She read it aloud annually, every word of it, on July fourth. Animated family discussions always followed her reading.

Today, even decades after her death, her children continue to get together to carry on this value-driven tradition without needing to be coaxed or reminded. In so doing, they honor one of their mother's cherished values and, at the same time, celebrate their mother. She didn't *write* a Legacy Document, but she knew with certainty that the particular set of values in the Declaration of Independence had become as alive and vital to her family as it was to her, and that brought her great satisfaction during her lifetime. Even after her death, there are generations now that include not only her children but also her grandchildren, whose reading and conversation about the Declaration of Independence creates an enduring legacy from one generation to another in this family.

Later generations are often fascinated by, and interested in, the traditions and habits of earlier generations and the stories that were important to their members. This is particularly true if later generations can understand what the driving force was behind each event. Since all people have stories that are unique to them, and each story is precious, traditions can often develop once the stories are shared. The telling is not exclusively the province of the story; if it were, it would simply be memoir. What a Legacy Document portrays, in addition to its explicit story, is the author's personal value or values that underlie the tale and are being passed down to newer generations. *It is the inclusion and amplification of these values that help to characterize a Legacy Document.* In the course of both telling a story and attributing a cherished value to the story's action, you assure yourself that it is not just your stories, but also your values, that will be known and carried forward as part of the inheritance. These values, therefore, are able to live on, can continue, even beyond your own years.

While you are preparing a Legacy Document, you have an opportunity to reflect on two things in particular: what you represent and what you value most in your life. You also have the opportunity, if you choose to take advantage of it, to make changes in the way you are living. Here's an example.

IS IT EVER TOO LATE TO CHANGE?

I was approached to do some short-term family therapy with Judith, a healthy, sixty-eight-year-old woman who had retired from her practice as a corporate lawyer four months earlier. With time on her hands, Judith had decided to write what she referred to as a "Legacy Document, a letter," and she came to me for guidance in her process.

"I'm way too young and healthy to need a will," she said, "even only an Ethical Will," she added parenthetically, as she smiled. "I just want to write a letter for down the road a while. . . . We could call the document a Legacy Letter!"

We worked for a couple of sessions discussing the things in life that she valued highly and held most dear. Judith was clear that family, not the law, was the fulcrum of her life. Divorced for many years, she lived alone and at a distance from both her son and her daughter and their families. Judith had five grandchildren and told me stories about them, but when I asked things like, "How tall is the eldest boy?" whom she described as loving basketball, she had no idea.

This led us to talk about her visits to see "the kids," that is, her own children. It turned out that Judith visited the family of each child once a year for a long weekend in their home, and "everyone" came to her house for Christmas every third year. (This pattern reflected the requisite "fair" or "equitable" numbers of visits devised sometimes in families of divorce, like her own.)

What I was observing, and Judith began to see for herself as we talked, was that her ostensible values and her actual life were very much out of sync with each other. She had the opportunity, now that she was retired and "only" sixty-eight, to take a look at what she said she valued most in her life, and to ask herself privately if the way she was living her life sufficiently reflected those values.

In Judith's case, she recognized that she was not living out her values in ways that her children were able to recognize. That came as a surprise to her, and it was certainly not pleasant. But it wasn't irresolvable. Judith quickly embarked on writing a letter for her Legacy Document and, even more important, before her letter was finished, she increased the frequency of her visits to her family. Despite some intense initial trepidation, she was thrilled that she was welcomed, not rebuffed as she had feared. In fact, her son's wife made a point of telling her just how much everyone looked forward to and enjoyed her more frequent visits.

As you read this chapter, you will have the option to decide whether developing a Legacy Document suits you. Those of you who choose to attempt one, of whatever sort feels most comfortable for you, can begin in any place and any way that feels right for you. You will see that you, too, have the opportunity to discern if your actions are truly reflective of your purported values, the ones you want to hand down as part of your individual legacy. Whether they are consistent or are not, accept the fact that recognition is the very first step on the way to change. I encourage every one of you to take that first step. Like Judith, you have the opportunity to see and correct any disparities between what you say matters to you and what your actions demonstrate you care most about.

I REPEAT THE QUESTION: WHAT ACTUALLY IS A LEGACY DOCUMENT?

As you begin to learn about and define the nature and purpose of a legacy, remember: *A Legacy Document is a personal, moral document, not a legal document.* Most people go to an attorney to write their Last Will and Testament, have it witnessed as they sign it, and file it safely away, frequently in their lawyer's offices, to be revised if needed, or to be readily accessed after death.

In contrast, the drafting of a Legacy Document is generally a personal matter, one that might be created on your own, in a writing group of some sort, perhaps individually in therapy, or even in a therapy group. How the document is saved is also a matter of personal choice. In some instances, it's saved with other documents on a computer, or printed out and saved in a physical file cabinet with an appropriate label on its manila folder, such as *Legacy Document* or *For My Grandchildren*. It may be stashed in a safe deposit box or even a household safe. Sometimes, as in my family, the document is read aloud by the Initiator at a family reunion or holiday get-together. Once you've taken the first step and put your thoughts on paper, the decisions that follow regarding what to do with the documents are also entirely your own. In writing groups or workshops, people often discuss possibilities they're considering for the safekeeping and ultimate presentation of their personal Legacy Document. Although you can't have that conversation when reading a book on your own, here's an exercise that *can* help you make thoughtful decisions.

EXERCISE: WHAT TO DO WITH YOUR LEGACY DOCUMENT ONCE IT'S WRITTEN

Let yourself imagine that you have just finished writing your Legacy Document, and you are pleased with it. As you read these questions, make some notes for yourself so you can be sure the document will be handled in the way that you intend. Your notes can include the answers to these questions and any others you think of:

1. Who, if anyone, would you like to have see and/or hear your Legacy Document *now*?
2. Is there anyone you'd like *not* to show or read it to at this time?
3. Do you think your answer to the second question will change? If so, can you predict why, when, and how?
4. Is your Legacy Document intended to be a personal document just for one specifically identified person whom you will identify now? Or is it for more than one person? If so, go ahead and identify them, as well.
5. Does it matter to you who will read your Legacy Document, or when?

You may have noticed that I did not mention, in the above list of questions, anything about how your Legacy Document might be responded to by the people you intend or hope to have read it. There's a reason for that omission; it's not an oversight. *You* are welcome and able to choose to write a Legacy Document, but it is binding on no one. You choose to write it. If you are planning to have it distributed according to your wishes after your death, the recipients of your Legacy Document will have the right to choose to read it or not. That's part of the reality of a document that consists of a moral inheritance, not a legal one. This Legacy Document's intention is simply to be a concrete presentation of memories, stories, love, and learning, any or all of which you will have documented and made available to future generations. The choice is entirely your own as to whether you want to offer your personal Legacy Document to *anyone* during your lifetime or distribute it only to those identified family members and/or friends who are alive after your death.

FOR THE LAST TIME: WHAT IS A LEGACY DOCUMENT?

Legacy Documents are a twenty-first-century creation and not typically subject to criticism either as a contemporary expression of egotism or narcissism or as psychobabble. Today, Legacy Documents are increasingly popular, both with the Initiators who create them and with the Listeners who receive them. Their formats are likely to be just as diverse as the stories and other legacies that are apt to be offered.

A contemporary Legacy Document can appear in any number of potential styles. Historically, we understand the Legacy Document to have been *either* verbal or written, and today, still, the document might be presented in either format. However, a Legacy Document certainly does not have to rely on the written word. A contemporary Legacy Document is frequently intended to transmit *spiritual or moral values* handed down from one generation (yours) to those in the future: from you, for example, to a child or grandchild—either one you already know or one who is not yet even conceived. Because the document serves, in some instances, to transmit legacies such as information, beliefs, values, and stories, in the casual writing style of a letter, sometimes people refer to it not as a "Legacy Document," but as a *Legacy Letter,* a term that some think sounds slightly younger and lighter. That seemed to be the case for Judith, the retired attorney whose story I related earlier in this chapter.

EXERCISE: IDENTIFY VALUES THAT MATTER TO YOU

Part 1

As a warm-up to the *possibility* of devising your own Legacy Document, let's start by thinking about, and then creating, a Values List. Randomly identify and write down all the values you can think of (things like beauty, truth, justice, commitment, and so on). Give yourself five minutes to create this values list.

- When that time is up, take a serious look at your list, and see which of the words are honestly most important to you.
- Which words are basic to how you live your life? In this context, you may want to add some value-driven words that you've omitted.
- Work with this list until you have a new, shortened list made up of the ten words that best reflect the values that define who you are, as well as why and how those values are reflected in the ways you've lived your life until now.

Take a break if you'd like, and come back to this exercise when you feel ready. If you're ready right now, just go ahead with part 2. It's going to require no more than fifteen minutes for writing.

Part 2

Looking at the ten most important words you've selected to represent your values on your Values List, and thinking in terms both of posterity and of stories for your Legacy Document, select up to five of your words. Using these chosen words, allow yourself to write a paragraph-length story that will convey some information about you and about your moral or spiritual values. Limit this exercise to about 150–175 total words. Two examples follow.

Value Words: Beauty, Friendship, Independence, Happiness

Sample Story 1: "As a little girl, I heard that I'd been considered a **beauty** by the nurses in the hospital, right after my birth. Yet, my mother seemed to think I was funny looking and said so. My **independence** was so important to me because of her harsh words. And **friendships** mattered more to me than mirrors. It's hard to say why, but I think I knew my friends saw beneath my surface. Their acceptance of me, and my pride in having good friends, was a source of **happiness** for me."

Sample Story 2: "I was the oldest child in my family of three kids, and I couldn't wait to go to sleep-away camp, but my parents wouldn't send me until I was eight. That seemed to me like a very long time to wait. Once I started, I spent all my summers at camp until I was nineteen. I was a city kid; the lake and trees and wildflowers that were all over the camp property were my **happiness**. I loved all this natural **beauty** totally! Camp was the best part of my life. It's where I developed **friendships** and learned about myself in ways I think were unique and meaningful in shaping me. As a camper, I had to work with other kids and my counselors. Being part of a camp group helped me develop my **independence**! Camp felt safe. At the end of August, we'd get on the bus to go back home, and everyone was sad."

Neither sample is a *perfect* story, but each is someone's actual first draft for this assignment; each serves here as an example for you. The next step is for you to write your own value-driven story in 150–175 words, as you exercise the muscles you'll need if you choose to develop your own personal Legacy Document in any fashion.

YOUR LEGACY DOCUMENT'S FORM CAN BE AUDIOVISUAL

Ellen Fisher-Turk, a photographer and coach in New York City, guides her clients to select ten (often family-related) photographs that are especially meaningful for them. In her groups, she encourages members to use each of the photographs as a separate prompt, and from them, to weave stories that serve as a composite audiovisual Legacy Document for each person.

The forms of these documents might be generated from *any* kind of graphic art, including photographs, film, paintings, or documentaries. If written, the range can be from prose to poetry and unlimited in length, taking into consideration your recipient's needs as Listener, as well as your own needs as the source of information, the Initiator (or in this situation, the storyteller). Feel free to let your imagination flow and create something unique, a Legacy Document in a form of your own.

Speaking of graphic art forms of Legacy Documents, I worked with a group of writers, each of whom decided to ask a grandchild to collaborate with them on their Legacy Document. They had varied ideas for the actual document, ranging from illustrated poetry to a very literate children's book— the kind that would be moving to a reader of any age from about eight years through adult. This book focused primarily on the enduring value of love. Its author's powerful words, repeated several times, were "Humans die; love does not." This contention was illustrated by an elementary school–age grandchild in intense watercolors. Of course, this idea, or value, is not for everyone. I cite it only to give you another idea of ways graphic art can be used to create Legacy Documents and to stimulate your thinking (while you may be building or strengthening a relationship with a grandchild).

WHY NOT WRITE A MEMOIR
INSTEAD OF A LEGACY DOCUMENT?

If you choose to create a Legacy Document, it will be with the intention that the *stories you tell will share and explicitly portray your values. You'd describe things you've done, and reveal yourself, in the context of your values.* Ultimately, you hope that each value-driven story will be remembered, and that it will serve as a model for the beliefs and behavior of future generations in your family or friendship line. The stories that are told in a memoir, on the other hand, are very simply *plot-driven* stories.

In a sense, the story told in a memoir is intended to interest, educate, or amuse the reader. The same story told in the context of a Legacy Document may cover the identical material, but it highlights the values involved even more than the plot or action. In the Legacy Document, your story conveys—emphasizes, in fact—"*why* I did what I did," not just "here are the interesting *facts* of what I did." As you work with chapter 9 you will be able to discriminate for yourself which values and what content you would choose to emphasize in a personal Legacy Document if you decide to work on one, very much as Kristina McMorris's grandfather did.

9

Ready, Set, Go:
Create Your Personal Legacy Document

I dwell in possibility. . . .

—Emily Dickinson, American Poet (1830–1886)

If you're feeling rather confident that you'd like to explore the *possibility* of creating a Legacy Document of your own, this chapter is your resource. In it, you'll continue to set the stage for creating the document of your choice. In chapter 8, you explored what a Legacy Document is and is not, and how to identify some of the values that have informed your life, values that you'd like future generations to hear about and remember in your personal Legacy Document. You're going to continue exploring, here, through some additional, written "how-to" exercises and stories. The end result will be material you can transform into the basis for your Legacy Document if that continues to be your goal.

EXERCISE: FORMING ONE
SEGMENT OF YOUR LEGACY DOCUMENT

This exercise will take you about thirty minutes initially. Ideally, you'll be able to be uninterrupted while you work on it. See if you can set yourself up to work without being subject to interference of any kind.

Begin by listing in your journal all the decades you've lived in so far: single numbers, teens, twenties, thirties, forties, and so on. Head a page for each decade.

Take the time to review your life, decade by decade. Select *one achieve-ment* or more in each decade that you are especially pleased by, proud of, or happy that you've accomplished. Take some time as you identify these, and allow yourself to really **be** there again, as each decade and achievement comes into memory. (If you're in your fifties, you'll have at least six achievements, and in your eighties, at least nine.) A reminder: "achievements" include ac-complishments that everyone could recognize, like the book you wrote or award you won, but they also include less obvious material, like your delicious chicken soup, or your devoted friends. Aspects of relationships often fall into the less obvious achievements and are worth considering valuable and being designated as such. Make notes on your journal pages to help you keep track of these decades of accomplishments as you review them.

Next step, looking at your list, select just one of these achievements to write about at greater length. Choose an achievement that serves to amplify a value that you hold dear and see as representative of many things in your life. Tell a story about this accomplishment, the value it is related to, and why that matters to you. Did it just occur to you, for example, to be funny? Or was good humor a value that you recognized in your mom or dad or a sibling, cousin, grandparent, and so on? As you saw them live it out and realized how they considered it important, perhaps you emulated them and then "owned this quality or value" for yourself when you discovered how well humor (our ex-ample here) served you in the world. You may also want to consider and write about what this value, as well as its related achievement, might mean for your family and/or friends in terms of your values and any influence on their values.

You might, alternatively, have succeeded in breaking with a pattern in your family (or friendship circle) and that might be the single most important achievement of your life to date. Your family members, for example, may always have lived in a small town in Minnesota, but you went to college in Minneapolis and chose to live there afterward, enjoying the big city, life in an apartment, and all the academic and cultural opportunities this large city offers. That's an achievement to value and talk about in terms of what it meant to you, and perhaps even what you had to give up in order to continue in this lifestyle.

Here's another example: If your value had to do with being competitive and winning and your achievement was an Olympic gold medal, what makes competing worthwhile for you? Why is it a value you hope people you love will recognize and even hold dear for themselves, as well? In your experience or opinion, are there also pitfalls, or caveats, you connect to this drive to win, this sense of competitiveness?

Spend some time writing about the quality that was the underpinning of your chosen achievement. Take a look at and describe how your own use of that quality was a particularly outstanding value in your life. Why has it remained valuable to you? Remember: You're writing about a major achievement in any one decade of your life to date and the value that made this accomplishment possible. Go ahead and write until you are satisfied with the effort and think you've begun something that will be worth sharing in time. Recognize that you are identifying this first value that will serve as a cornerstone of your Legacy Document, and do it justice as you proceed to work with it. When you're satisfied that you're done, you're welcome to choose another value to work on in a similar way. Remember that writing this document provides opportunities for you to see attributes in yourself that you may have taken for granted or not noticed at all. Feel free both to learn about yourself through these exercises and to appreciate the qualities and values that you are discovering.

EXERCISE: DEVELOPING A SECOND LEGACY DOCUMENT SEGMENT

This writing prompt is meant to go a little bit more quickly than the previous one. For most people, it takes about twenty minutes to think through and write about, but that's only a guide. If you need more time, do take it.

Think about the *teachings* each decade of your life to date has brought you. They may be secular, spiritual, artistic, professional, athletic—teachings of any kind at all so long as you value them.

Think, and then write, about how you incorporated any one particular teaching into your life and what it has meant to you.

Finally, consider: What has the role of this teaching been as you've aged? Did it remain important? Become more important? Become less important despite its valuable role in earlier decades? This is pertinent to you at any age; you don't need to be eighty or ninety to reflect on something!

Ken's Example

Ken, who is nearing fifty, identified an academic teaching in the second decade of his life as one he has particularly valued: he studied Italian for three years in high school and was ultimately able to speak, understand, and read it. In our group, Ken was a little shy about openly acknowledging how he initially incorporated this teaching into his life, but eventually he told us. His family was originally from Italy and he, Ken, was the eldest of his three siblings, all of whom were born in the United States. His grandparents and parents used to jabber away in Italian, particularly when they didn't want the kids to know what they were discussing. Once he'd learned a little

Italian, he was motivated to listen in and see what he could understand, never letting on that he had become sufficiently proficient to follow their conversations! For a full year, he got away with this subterfuge, but one day, he remembered laughing out loud when they were mocking a particularly tall aunt whom no one especially liked. The family stared at him as he tried unsuccessfully to stifle his laughter. "Ah, well," he thought, "that I totally understood and spoke Italian was my great secret—while it lasted." And he continued to think that, alone in his room, during his twenty-minute time-out!

As for how else Ken was able to incorporate learning Italian, his teaching of choice, into his life, and how it had become more and less important as he aged, Ken was clear. He grew to love the Italian language and his heritage and spent a gap year in Italy after college before going on to graduate school and following a career path that was totally unrelated to Italy or the Italian language. Even so, the importance of Italy and the country's language remained prominent throughout his adult life, always a source of pleasure to him and to his own family (wife and children) as well. Vacations were primarily to the Italian countryside, and he's even considering Lucca as the location for his ultimate retirement—if his wife will agree to go there with him!

Lucy's Example

Lucy chose rollerblading as her primary achievement. It was something she had worked hard to learn one spring in the third decade of her life, about two years before she married. In fact, she met her prospective husband as she was leaving her ninth rollerblading lesson—she couldn't help but mention to the group in which she was working.

Incorporating the hobby of rollerblading into her life was easy at first—Lucy did it daily in good weather—and then talked and thought about it vividly and frequently through the winter. However, four years after she'd become a rollerblading enthusiast, Lucy was married and pregnant. Rollerblading took up a significant position in her memories, but she never really went back to it as an active sport. Skating and rollerblading both became less physically present in her more adult life, as she described in the group, but "the fun, even the thrill of it" has stayed vivid in her memory and remains important in that sense. So she chose rollerblading as a teaching that she values, even though "I'd absolutely never have predicted that. And I can see my grandkids being skeptical about me as a rollerblading 'dervish,'" as she put it. Nonetheless, the memory of how much fun it brought her, and the delight of speed and intention and coordination . . . these she values, even treasures. Also, the recognition that the only part of this activity that was competitive was with herself. She always wanted to do better than the last time. Her goal was to become increasingly proficient. Lucy wanted to incorporate all of this insight into her Legacy Document, without question.

EXERCISE: IDENTIFY REGRETS, IF ANY

Take a few quiet minutes to review the decades of your life one more time. This time as you scan, think about whether you are aware of any regrets at all. Are there things that happened, either by choice or by default, throughout the course of your life that, in retrospect, you regret? Many? A few?

Using the two stories that follow as possible prompts for writing this part of your Legacy Document, let yourself revive your memories and the emotions prompted by them. Listen to any regrets, losses, or recollections that come to mind, and write about them now, with an eye toward possibly including these thoughts in the Legacy Document you are creating.

Jonathan's Example

Jonathan married in his twenties, choosing a woman who he felt would be a wise choice as his wife. He liked her, thought she was attractive, and knew she came from a good family; she was bright and had many friends. He felt she was a better candidate than any of the other women he was dating and, as he approached his thirties, he was becoming ready to marry.

Jonathan and his wife had three children together but ultimately divorced. He then married a woman who was the love of his life, but after nearly three decades together, she died. This exercise distressed him. He wrote, "I have so many regrets! Life is much shorter than we realize at twenty. I made a business decision about my first wife, and I was unfair to both of us, as well as to the woman I ultimately married. Follow your *heart* when love and marriage is involved. That's what I want to say in my Legacy Document to my kids. I've always regretted making the wrong initial choice. So many people were hurt."

Cheryl's Example

Cheryl described herself as having chosen to live "an unconventional life in the 'burbs' of metropolitan New York City." She had four children, was divorced while they lived at home with her and went to public schools, and shortly thereafter, became "actively woman-identified" (translation: she was gay). There were many secretive, painful years for her, she described, when she felt that it was important that her relationships be kept hidden. What Cheryl described as part of her regrets wasn't her choice of "female candidates for her affection" as she said in her writing, but rather in "feeling I had to keep my choices hidden—from my parents, while they still were alive, from my kids, and especially from my ex-husband. I was so afraid he'd be vindictive in some way or other, and try to take the children away from me. He found it so easy to call me an unfit mother for behaviors that were far more conventional."

With the opportunity to write a values-driven Legacy Document, this section about regrets opened the chance for Cheryl to examine why she had done what she did and regretted: imposing secrecy on her feelings and actions. As she wrote and thought about that time period, these new realizations helped her gradually to become considerably kinder to herself than had been her habit. What's more, she understood that "love was beneath all the things I did, my actions and my silences, and I still believe in love and loving. That's what I want to reflect in my Legacy Document when I put this material to use."

You don't need to agree with Jonathan or Cheryl or Lucy. You only need to observe the ways in which they each chose to reflect both life experience and values in a Legacy Document. I expect that's what many of you will do—use your Legacy Document to *reflect on*, as well as to describe, both your stories and your values. First for yourself, but ultimately, for posterity.

FORGIVENESS AS A COMPONENT OF YOUR LEGACY DOCUMENT

When Pope Francis concluded his first visit to the United States in 2015, news commentators and people who had heard his remarks, either in person or on television or radio, often spoke about the graciousness of this very special man. He was thought to have exemplified someone who does, to and for others, what he would hope they can do to and for him, and to and for one another. We understand that Pope Francis is no stranger to forgiveness. Regardless of your own religious, spiritual, or ethical predispositions, see if you can be comfortable with whatever you do or don't feel, being no stranger to forgiveness, as you approach this exercise. In order to stimulate an exploration of still another value that might have a place in a Legacy Document if you want to write one, consider the following exercise.

EXERCISE: CONSIDER YOUR "FORGIVENESS MUSCLES"

1. On a clean page in your journal, create two vertical columns. Head the left one **People I have hurt in my lifetime** and the right one **People who have hurt me**.
2. Again, review the decades of your life and write any names in the appropriate list. Have you already made closure with one or more of the people in either column? If not, would you be interested in forgiving any of these people, or making changes in one or more of these relationships, either directly in writing or by talking, or perhaps simply in your own mind?

These questions raise still more questions. For instance, once you've determined who it is you'd choose to forgive, *how will you do that?* If it's yourself you'd like to forgive, it's a particularly difficult question: How *will* you do that?

Jean's Example

A mom in her early fifties, Jean had been diagnosed with breast cancer, and she felt that it was imperative that she go into surgery without any "unfinished business." She telephoned each of her twenty something-year-old daughters separately and explained this to them. Then, despite feeling very anxious, particularly during her conversation with her elder daughter, she absolutely made herself ask, "Is there anything I've done that you find hard to forgive me for?" There was a pause.

"Umm, yeah," the elder daughter said. "But it was long ago."

"Go ahead, even so," Jean said, feeling more than nervous.

"You shrunk my Meronas, the first time you washed my only pair. And you never replaced them, Mom," her daughter revealed.

Jean's reaction was confusion. She really didn't know whether to laugh or cry. She'd totally forgotten about this. Clearly, her daughter had not. Well, they talked. Each helped the other understand why they'd done what they'd done and felt what they'd felt, and before long it was okay to laugh together about the episode.

So how might this story about the shrunken Meronas help you think and write about forgiveness? As you make your own lists and consider talking with anyone from whom you want to ask forgiveness, recognize that what's important to one person isn't necessarily important to, or even remembered by, the other. Be very sure that you take this into account before you write or telephone or go for tea or coffee with someone, intending to ask for forgiveness.

Take these thoughts and sort out the *values* you consider important (worth attempting to pass on to future generations). Next, tell a story that illuminates these values, as part of your Legacy Document.

EXERCISE: TAKE A MOMENT
TO REFLECT ON THE FUTURE

Here's where any Legacy Document can get into trouble. If and when you want to give directions to the generations that follow you about how they "should" live their lives, you are most likely going to turn them off. You don't want to do that, of course. Instead, keep telling *your stories* (and feel free to use good humor like Jean's daughter did about her Meronas). Let the value-filled stories speak for themselves. Your readers or the recipients of your Legacy Document may or may not live their lives as you've been living yours. They may not be guided by the very same needs, values, or circumstances. Ideally, a Legacy Document doesn't attempt to force any thoughts or behaviors on anyone else. Rather, the contemplation of a Legacy Document offers the opportunity for you to learn about yourself in the process of creating it. Further, it provides an opportunity for you to be a bit better known by expanding the audience of this knowledge, these stories. Remember: the messages of a Legacy Document are likely to be clear, but they are not binding.

With this in mind and if you've chosen to create a Legacy Document of your own, you may be ready to make a first draft, one that is on its way to being useful for you to be better, or differently, known by subsequent generations.

At this point, it's time to reflect on and pay attention to any of the things you've overlooked as you've read and thought about all the material in this book so far. I hope you'll take advantage of the opportunity to notice your own accidentally overlooked thoughts as well as any of your stumbling blocks—the ones you've already run into and the ones you want to be mindful of and prevent. In chapter 10, I'll do just that: convey my experience as well as telling stories about possible or actual obstacles to a successful communication. This is followed in chapter 11 by some of my own reflections as I have reviewed the introduction and the first ten chapters of *Your End of Life Matters*. I've included ideas or concepts I want to share with you but hadn't yet found the "right place" for in those earlier chapters. Read on and see what thoughts and reflections of your own get stimulated as well.

10

Ask Yourself, What Obstacles Could Possibly Get in the Way of My Conversation?

Difficulties mastered are opportunities won.

—Winston S. Churchill, British Statesman (1874–1965)

$\mathcal{D}$eciding how to begin this chapter about obstacles or stumbling blocks to the work of talking about end-of-life matters in itself became an obstacle of sorts to writing it. With Churchill's words in mind, I set out to "master" this difficulty. I concluded ultimately that I had an opportunity—to begin the chapter by identifying three of the most likely sources of obstacles. With that accomplished, I would move on to present several illustrative stories, beginning with a candid, personal one.

Potential obstacles fall within three categories, any one of which might deter a successful end-of-life conversation:

1. Obstacles that seem just to "come out of the blue"
2. Obstacles that derive from the Initiator
3. Obstacles that originate from one or more Listener(s)

As we progress through this chapter, I'll explore examples of all three categories of obstacles so you can learn to recognize in advance, and perhaps prevent, some of the more commonplace obstacles. I emphasize, in the exercises and situations presented throughout this book, that the *opportunity* most often sought is for a Listener to agree to be responsible for carrying out the Initiator's end-of-life wishes, during the Initiator's lifetime and after his or her death. Reading further, it is easy to recognize the kinds of difficulties that are hard, maybe impossible, to master.

AN UNANTICIPATED MEMORY

As I began to write this chapter, focused as it is on a variety of obstacles that might prevent an Initiator from effectively communicating end-of-life matters, an unanticipated memory from a recent event kept cropping up. I'm choosing to tell you about it, rather than allowing it to keep knocking impertinently on the door of my memory bank and keeping me from writing.

My Obstacle-Related Memory (Representing Category 1)

I was a guest at a December holiday gathering in suburban New York City in 2016, the year I was close to finishing writing the first full draft of this book. Images of the early part of that evening are the ones that persistently popped up in my memory, almost the way a writing prompt could work. For a while, this memory made it hard for me to do virtually anything except to remember my feelings of dread. It threatened to become a two-pronged obstacle to the completion of the manuscript, rather out of the blue at that. Although only momentarily, the memory of this experience got in the way of my writing schedule and had also briefly shaken my belief in the far-reaching validity of my material. How annoying! Perhaps also, how human of me! Here's the story.

This party's guests ranged widely in age, from approximately forties to seventies. I knew and liked the hosts, who were professional colleagues of mine, but to my surprise, I wasn't familiar with any of the other guests. Hors d'oeuvres circulated, and drinks were available. And, as people do conventionally at holiday parties, we exchanged pleasantries and discussed where we'd be spending the coming winter holidays. Then the randomness of the evening changed.

An initial activity was announced and carefully described. It was intended to involve absolutely every guest. It would probably last for more than an hour during which cocktails and hors d'oeuvres were still passed, so the group's members would continue to stay pretty much in one place. Arthur, one of the hosts, had planned and organized this activity, describing us as a rather disparate group and hoping we'd find it interesting to learn what kind of work each attendee was involved in; it might even be good for networking. My first thought was that it would be a good idea to leave now, before I was trapped for as long as this might last! Ultimately though, my curiosity took over, and I decided to stay on, even though this "party game" felt a lot like a category one (out of the blue) *obstacle* to my planned early retreat so I could resume writing.

Questions and answers flowed. Most of the assembled guests seemed to enjoy the prospect of having a couple of minutes in the spotlight, plus a sense of genuine interest in one another was building. The guests included therapists, writers, actors, travel agents, teachers, a couple of CEOs, and political activists; one person was starting a hedge fund and another worked at a tech start-up. Some second-career people included a man who was changing from internal medicine as a hospitalist to a concierge medical practice. It turned out indeed to be a very suburban Manhattan, dynamic, high-power group.

When it was my turn to speak, I explained succinctly what this book was about and what I would like the outcome to be for each reader, ending by saying something like: "I hope that the book's readers will follow the example of my parents and talk successfully about their own end-of-life matters. Or perhaps it'll be more appropriate for them to prompt their own parents or friends to do this for themselves." I was extremely uncomfortable and taken aback when a prolonged silence followed my remarks.

"What just happened?" I asked eventually, looking around the newly quiet room rather anxiously. I held my breath, fearing it was the topic that had engendered the silence, and maybe I should never have mentioned it. Or worse, maybe no one ever would want to know more about this material. (Fear, another unexpected obstacle to my writing, felt like it was rearing its head.)

"Bravo!" one of the older male guests bellowed, and clapped. "Do we ever need your book!" He looked around the room, and asked, "May I?" As heads nodded, he began to talk about his father's recent death after a prolonged stint of illness and surgeries including a tracheotomy, and his own abject sense of not knowing what to do.

"I wish we'd had your book to reference before Dad was ever sick! It was an awful time for my dad. And for me. I certainly don't want that to happen to us again if my mom starts to fail!" he continued.

His wife, very gently, put her hand on his arm and said, "Or to our kids someday! We need to talk in both directions. Yikes! Suddenly we're in the 'Sandwich Generation'!"

An animated, fairly disorganized discussion followed, and for much of it, I just tried to hear what was being said. I was stunned and very relieved. No obstacle, unless my imagination counts. But I was also surprised and pleased, as people spontaneously tossed around who they thought they needed either to tell or hear from and how they felt at the prospect of actually being part of a conversation of this sort, in either position. It didn't seem to matter to anyone if they would be (in my terms) Initiators, Listeners, or both! It was the "safety" of having told trustworthy people what they wanted them to know that mattered. Many said they felt they'd be better able to get on with living life as fully as possible. (I certainly agreed with that, as you know already.)

The consensus surprised and excited me. This social group of people really responded positively to what the book I'd described has to say! Given the vital conversation that followed, the party quickly stopped feeling like any sort of obstacle to my progress on this book. Rather, it served as the source of a new story to begin the obstacles chapter, as well as of ideas about exercises and conversation prompts.

With no further obstacles I'm personally aware of at the moment, join me in the exercises that follow. They call on *your* imagination.

EXERCISE: IMAGINE OBSTACLES

As with the earlier exercises, you'll want to have your journal (notepad, writing implement, tablet, laptop, etc.) and a timer of some kind at hand as you begin. Set your timer for twenty minutes before you read further. I'm going to suggest several questions for you to reflect on and answer. If you don't have either time or inclination to answer all of them, that's perfectly all right. You may choose to spend all of your time writing a response to just one because it's most important or interesting to you. This is *your* exercise; use it so that it can be of benefit to you.

Part 1

Read through the following directions so that you will actually remember them as you *do* this exercise:

1. Seat yourself comfortably in a chair, preferably one with arms, on which you will rest your own arms. (If your chair does not have arms, simply allow your arms to hang down at your sides, touching the rest of your body as little as possible.)
2. Knowing that some noises are almost inevitable, let yourself decide that when you hear them, you'll easily let the sounds go as you allow yourself to drift into your quiet, private, internal space. Gently, close your eyes.
3. Allow yourself to see, imagine, or feel that you are one of the guests at the holiday gathering I've just described to you. What will you say, in terms of what *you* are doing these days? What were you thinking or feeling when you read how the discussion turned after I spoke? Already knowing the basic premise of my book, how is it for you when you consider my articulated wishes for this book: "*I hope that readers will follow the example of my parents and talk successfully about their own end-of-life matters. Or perhaps prompt their own parents or friends to do the same thing for themselves.*" Allow yourself to analyze your own thoughts and feelings as you read these words. Are you considering taking on one of those roles? Are there obstacles in your own way?

What are they? And in which of the three categories do they fit? Will you have to create a new category to contain your obstacle(s)?

- Are you curious and open to thinking about having a conversation like this of your own?
- Are you much more interested in making sure that your parents or older friends talk to you about *their* end-of-life matters?
- Are you even less inclined, and wishing that you'd never heard word one about this possible conversation?
- Are your thoughts and feelings jumbled? Do you feel put on the spot when guided to figure out your answer?
- Anything else?

Spend the rest of the time reflecting or meditating (or both) until your timer goes off. When it does, slowly open your eyes, shut off the timer, and immediately jot down any thoughts, feelings, or other notes you want to be sure to remember.

Allow yourself to spend a minute or two coming back to the room before moving on to the second part of this exercise.

Part 2

Sit comfortably with your journal. Set your timer again, also for twenty minutes, and with the same directions as before.

1. How did you feel about the earlier twenty minutes of reflection and meditation? (If you want more time for any of those questions, you're welcome to take it now, and then turn to these when you're ready to move on.)
2. Were you able to see, imagine, or feel a response to the brief description of my book project as if you were a guest at that gathering? (Reminder: my remarks were, *"That readers will follow the example of my parents and talk successfully about their own end-of-life matters. Or perhaps prompt their own parents or friends to do the same thing for themselves."*)
3. Where did your thoughts take you?
4. Were there obstacles for you, having to do with being involved in this process of a conversation about end-of-life matters? What were those obstacles? Is it possible for you to overcome any or all of the obstacles you've recognized during the meditation?
5. Allow yourself to write about the obstacles in some detail during this twenty-minute reflective exercise. If your mind wants to wander, go ahead and let it, and then make some notes about what it was you were thinking about.

SYLVIA'S STORY

An Initiator-Driven Obstacle (Representing Category 2)

A CAVEAT: Pay attention to communicating your end-of-life thoughts and intentions with absolute clarity. Express only those thoughts you consciously intend to convey.

"Sylvia's story" that follows was brought to my attention by an attorney who had heard me lecture, and who talked with me briefly about his lingering discomforts about this particular case. He thought we both might learn something from it.

His client was Sylvia, a sixty-five-year-old widow of about five years. He was her family's attorney, and had helped the couple draw up the couple's will while both were in good health a number of years back. At that time, although they didn't use these terms, Sylvia and Arnold (wife and husband) were mutually Initiators and Listeners for one another, and the ultimate distribution of their assets would be shared equally between their two children and their families. They had chosen not to discuss wills with either child, nor any other end-of-life details.

Arnold pre-deceased Sylvia. She followed through on many of his suggestions. For instance, shortly after his death, she took over their newer car, his convertible, and sold her SUV. She hired an organizer and got rid of Arnold's books and papers and clothing, making room to spread out her own belongings and be very comfortable. (Sylvia had always felt at a loss for space, while Arnold would tell anyone who listened that what she was at a loss for was organizational skills.) After a while, Sylvia wanted to draw up a new will of her own. She set up a meeting with their attorney and brought along their daughter, also a lawyer, but a litigator with no experience in family law or trusts and estates, to sit in silently on the meeting. Sylvia said this was so the daughter would know that the document was being created while she was of sound mind as well as body. She felt no need to bring her son into this. He lived at a distance from her, close to his wife's family, and Sylvia didn't feel very close to him. She felt she'd lost that branch to his wife's "side."

This is a good time for you to stop reading and, briefly, give some thought to Sylvia's situation and then do some journaling.

Exercise: What Would You Do Now, If You Were Sylvia?

This exercise should take you no longer than five to eight minutes, so go to the most comfortable place for you to journal, set a timer for yourself if you'd like, and then use some or all of these questions as your writing prompts.

Allow yourself to pretend that you are Sylvia. You've been widowed for five years, and it's time to revise your will. Ask yourself these three questions:

1. What might be the issues in your will that you are likely to feel most sensitive about?
2. What aspects of revising your will now might you be most anxious to "get right"?
3. What are the thoughts that cause you the most anxiety?

(Men, if you feel that it's helpful for you, reverse roles. Pretend Arnold is the survivor, and let it be your wife, Sylvia, who died first. The other facts and questions remain the same, whichever gender role you imagine yourself taking.)

Write your answers to whichever question(s) you've focused on before going any further in this story. In five to eight minutes, stop the writing exercise you are doing and return, please, to the story of Arnold and Sylvia, as it actually happened. Let's see if you were able to anticipate any of the obstacles Sylvia in fact came up against.

Sylvia's Story Continues: More Obstacles

In updating her will, Sylvia made changes that were contrary to Arnold's wishes, and the attorney never knew if Sylvia was purposely countermanding Arnold's will, or doing so inadvertently. This troubled the attorney, but he believed that his role in creating or amending wills was explicitly to take direction from the client, not to advocate for change. Even so, he feared that his silence may have inadvertently helped create an obstacle to the fair and equitable distribution of the remaining assets.

Twelve years later, Sylvia had a heart attack and died in her sleep. After trying to reach her by telephone for a bit over a day, her son became worried that he was unable to make contact. He drove the five hundred miles from his home to Sylvia's place in New Jersey. He used the house key hidden in a key rock, entered the premises, and found his mother's lifeless body. First he called 9-1-1 and then his sister.

A few days after the funeral, the children met with the attorney, who read aloud their mother's Last Will and Testament to her heirs. Again, the attorney found himself wondering if a mistake had been made. The daughter and her family were the recipients of two-thirds of everything that was left, while the son and his family had been left only one-third. A cruel blow to Sylvia's son, made even more painful because of his obvious concern for his mother and the shocks of the recent loss.

Turning to his sister, in distress, he asked if she was also surprised. Looking at the attorney first, she responded, "Hardly. I was here when she wrote it."

"And you allowed me to be treated like this?" her brother continued, in disbelief. "I can't believe it. Dad would never have wanted us treated this way!"

"Dad, however, had no say anymore. He died first," countered his sister.

The attorney concluded this story, shaking his head sadly. The family lawyer was deeply distressed, and said this experience caused him to rethink the way he counseled people writing wills.

Is That What Sylvia Had Intended?

You may be wondering if this was really what Sylvia had intended, and I certainly am, as was the attorney. But unless Sylvia had left explanatory letters, her intentions remain opaque, which is very sad for each of her surviving children and their families. Remember the "caveat" at the beginning of this story: *Pay attention to communicating your end-of-life thoughts and intentions with absolute clarity. Express only those thoughts you consciously intend to convey.*

Because resentments festered, Sylvia's legacy was either spoiled or exactly what she'd wanted, but none of us will ever know what she intended. Because of the daughter's silence as she witnessed the differences between this new will of her mother's and the original will agreed to by both parents, it's hard not to think she was happy about the unequal distribution of assets in her favor. Is this an example of a Listener-generated *obstacle*? Or was it Initiator-*intended and generated*?

We see ever more clearly what an Initiator's most important responsibility is: *Communicate your end-of-life matters with absolute clarity, whatever those matters may be! Do not allow lack of transparency on your part, as Initiator, to become an obstacle to your actual intentions.* A Listener's most important responsibility is to follow through with integrity once he or she has agreed to what is being asked. Listeners have the right to refuse the responsibility if and when they consider the Initiator's wishes to be unreasonable for them to agree to carry out. In this situation, Sylvia's daughter seems to also have had culpability. Her silence, her unwillingness to ask any question about her mother's intention with this two-thirds versus one-third distribution of assets may have created a second *obstacle* to the distribution outcome Sylvia intended.

From this story, we learn: *Communicate clearly! Ask Questions when you are not sure what is being asked of you as Listener (or attorney!).* Unclear, vague, or ambiguous directives might become obstacles to carrying out the intentions of the Initiator. In Sylvia's story, we are left without the clarity to know what she really intended in her heart.

SAM'S STORY

Unexpected Obstacles (Representing Category 1)

Not all people are either willing to have a conversation about end-of-life matters or capable of doing so. It could be either an Initiator or a Listener whose personality will most likely set up failure, not success, for the proposed end-of-life discussion we have been exploring.

Sam is a fascinating man who simply could be neither Listener nor Initiator. He is exceptionally bright, an excellent artist, and an even better cook. Happily married, he is nonetheless a loner. He has few friends, pets, or children. His relationship with his father was polite, but distant at best. He was successful in the corporate world, yet left it abruptly when he was in his mid-fifties.

Sam's initial conundrum was that, while he loved and respected his mother, he never loved his father and would never have agreed to serve as Listener to him, had he been asked. Nonetheless, because Sam is a highly ethical man, his goal, after his father first was widowed and then went on to become infirm himself, was to provide the man with the best care available, but to otherwise have virtually nothing to do with him. This, to his way of thinking, was an acceptable compromise. He was entirely unwilling to push the envelope any further. Sam did just as he planned, making certain that his dad's physical needs were met and his health protected as much as possible. Nevertheless, Sam chose to have almost no face-to-face interactions with his dad. Sam functioned for his father *as if* he were his Listener, but he wasn't, nor would he have consented to be.

What if Sam's father had ever attempted to initiate a discussion of his actual end-of-life matters? Sam would have rejected the premise and emphatically refused to participate as Listener in any such conversation. His intention would still have been to "*do the right thing*" but without any input from his dad as to what he himself wanted or thought of as "right" for himself. That would have been too intimate, and intimacy of this sort was anathema to Sam.

So let's move along to Sam himself as a prospective, official Listener—or Initiator. His wife, Eileen, knew about end-of-life conversations from the senior center where she took classes, participated in a book group, and occasionally had lunch. She was a friendly, social woman, and in that way, very much the opposite of her husband.

Eileen wanted them to discuss their own end-of-life matters together, and she hoped that Sam would eventually agree to be her official Listener, and she his. In truth, since they had no children and very few close friends, they were also one another's best choice. Well, the resounding *No!* that Sam spat out with venom as Eileen asked more than convinced her to go no further in trying to get to *yes* with Sam on this topic. It was obviously not a subject that was open to negotiation! For Eileen, that was an insurmountable, unexpected obstacle to her initial thoughts regarding a conversation. Case temporarily closed while Eileen reflected further.

MULTIPLE ROLES, MULTIPLE OBSTACLE POSSIBILITIES

The attorney's story about Sylvia let us see how ambiguity flowed from her role as solo Initiator. The new will she wrote after her husband's death made it impossible to determine where the obstacle sat. Sylvia had two distinctly different roles: initially she was a partnered-Initiator as well as her husband's Listener. Ultimately, she was a solo Initiator, without any Listener.

Sam, on the other hand, would not have allowed himself to be identified as Listener had his father asked that of him, nor would he do so for his wife. His clear response to Eileen's request, however, left no doubt about his relation to the *category three obstacle* he presented for her.

I'm going to present one more story with a multiple-role obstacle to carrying out the original Initiator's wishes. In Cookie's case, we again see a *category three obstacle* to an earlier agreement by the original Listener, but in the later, *category two* situation, as Cookie's role changed from Listener to Initiator, there was no ambiguity about her intention. The surviving spouse in this third story about obstacles appears to have chosen to subvert the agreed-upon wishes of her (second) husband following his death.

I'm speaking now of a family that was combined after one partner was widowed and one divorced. There were four children altogether, two girls from the husband's side and two girls from the wife's. The kids were well into high school when the families merged, and they were a lively bunch. There was an ongoing closeness that continued, even after college, through marriages, and the births of the members of the next generation.

The husband, Marvin, and wife, Cookie, were financially comfortable and traveled a lot, often buying pieces of art. One purchase was a painting, made at the suggestion of the eldest daughter, who had a serious interest in art and Asian artists. Her father said, after buying the painting and hanging it in the living room of their home, that this painting was hers, although it would be on display during their lifetime in their home, not hers. That was agreed upon and understood, even laughed at by the rest of the family, and specifically made reference to from time to time.

Marvin pre-deceased his second wife after a long and difficult illness. He had written a will while still in good health, but it omitted any mention of having given this significant piece of art as a gift, or to whom. Cookie, his primary survivor, knew exactly what he had intended to do with his assets; they'd both spoken often about this. She chose, however, to do something quite different in terms of the distribution of assets including their art collection, which the children only discovered after her subsequent death. That piece of Asian art became the primary object of contention between the children because, as it turned out, the painting had appreciated and become exceedingly valuable. Most ludicrous was how quickly the three children who had viewed the painting with disdain suddenly pronounced their love of it and each claimed having always wanted it.

Lawyers were engaged, and the litigation continued for years. I've lost touch with the family, so I have no idea what eventually happened, although it's hard to think the outcome, in the absence of a written document, was likely to be what Marvin intended—which had only been promised verbally, never included in a written directive. Obstacle number two: the deceased father turned out to be an Initiator who had been deceived by this wife, his Listener. Obstacle number three: as Listener for her husband, and then as his survivor, Cookie chose to create an entirely new set of wishes in which she never included the promises to her now deceased husband, the father of her two stepchildren.

Obstacles can and do sometimes come into play for both Initiators and Listeners. These instances may well sabotage the original intention of an end-of-life discussion. Let me report, however, that that happens much less often than successful completion and follow-through on these understandings, particularly when the *"willingness question"* (mentioned initially in chapters 3 and 5) has been addressed truthfully and is resolved. With that in place, Listener obstacles are rare.

EXERCISE: IDENTIFYING AND REMOVING OBSTACLES

This exercise provides an opportunity for you to review the groundwork you've established for your own communication about the end-of-life wishes that matter most to you. It provides a method for you to remove the obstacles or stumbling blocks that are likely to interfere with your conversation's success. You'll be able to recognize and either prevent or clear away many of the obstacles that might otherwise get in your way.

I suggest that you plan to allow at least fifteen minutes to move through the following exercise and to process your responses.

1. To begin, start a new page in your journal.
2. Head this page: **Goal: To effectively communicate my clearly thought-out end-of-life wishes**.
3. Draw a line down the middle of the page.
4. On the left side of the page, your subheading is **Obstacles**. Here you'll list any of the reasons you are currently aware of that will keep you from either getting started or moving forward and planning your conversation.
5. On the right side of the page, label your column with the subheading **Actions**. Here you can defeat your stumbling blocks, one by one, with actions you can take to clear the way for accomplishing your goal.
6. Either on the back of this page or on a new page, you'll want to create one more heading: **My Plan**.

After you've finished reading this whole book, this journal page is one you'll want to have marked so it's easy to find and refer to. You can use your notes in this exercise to create and then follow through with any written strategy you'll want, to help you as you make an end-of-life communication actually happen. The "My Plan" page, which may either have notes already or still be blank, can help you focus on the plan you want to create and put successfully into effect.

REFLECTIONS FOLLOW

The key to our thinking about obstacles is that we need to be conscious that they are possible, but know that most obstacles are within an Initiator's power to avoid, if one is willing to be honest and clear—with yourself as well as with your Listener(s). We will move on from the exploration of obstacles and head to chapter 11, which is about reflections—mine—as I look back over the book to this point and comment, adding some stories and even an exercise for you to do. I hope you will also participate in the process of recognizing and journaling about your own reflections on end-of-life conversations and legacies as you read chapter 11.

11

Reflections

Yes, in spite of all / Some shape of beauty moves away the pall
/ From our dark spirits.

—John Keats, English Poet (1795–1821)

*S*hortly after I'd entered into a formal contract with Rowman & Littlefield
for the publication of this book, my acquisitions editor offered a suggestion:
"I'd like to see some of your reflections on this material added in a separate
chapter." My compliance with that recommendation developed in ways that
surprised me initially, but ultimately formed the basis of the entire chapter
that you are about to read.

Months after I finished writing the story in chapter 5 of Grandpa Louie,
my maternal grandfather, I had a startling thought, a reflection. Although
I have no memory of either of my parents ever saying this to me directly, I
suddenly found myself considering the probability that they suffered terribly
from not knowing what my grandfather would have wanted when he was
hospitalized. They did not know anything about what was "the right thing"
for them to do on his behalf during his eight-week hospitalization in an intensive care unit without any hope of a full—or even partial—recovery.

My parents knew what it was costing them financially and emotionally
to be sure Grandpa Louie had private nurses around the clock and other
good care that was keeping him alive, plus their own daily visits. Was all of
this medical intervention what he would have chosen? They had no way of
knowing because the subject had never come up. Neither they nor my grandfather had given any thought to identifying end-of-life matters, especially
since my grandmother had died quickly and unexpectedly, a burden to no
one, prompting no "if only" at all. My father's parents each had had similarly
peaceful deaths. Frankly, my guess is that my grandfather, after surviving a

couple of heart attacks, thought the next one would take him when it happened. Nature has her ways. What was there that could possibly be useful to talk about? He preferred to smoke his cigar and have our nearly daily egg creams without "*depressing conversations.*"

Not once did my parents experience the benefits of the kind of informative and useful communication we have been discussing throughout this book. They had never listened in advance, gaining knowledge of either parental end-of-life matters or those of other close friends or family members, in return for which they might have given reassurances that they could be counted on to follow through as had just been described. No Initiator/Listener experiences for either of my parents—until they *initiated* their own conversation with me as their Listener.

As I reflected further, it seemed clear that the information my parents gave me, in what seemed like a well-organized although spontaneous telephone call, must literally have been germinating in their thoughts ever since my grandfather's death! I was both stunned and profoundly touched as that probable reality came alive in my mind. My parents, I have now recognized, once were candidates to be Listeners, but they never got that chance because of my grandfather's fall and subsequent untimely death. That life-changing experience made their decision crucial, many years later, to be the Initiators of their own conversation with me, leaving nothing to chance, no decisions for me to have to second-guess and worry about. Although they never mentioned it, I think it's clear that they knew how painful that experience could be.

Reflecting on this slice of family history, I realized that it was my grandfather's dying and death, not only a conversation with friends, that must have served as the genesis of my parents' telephone call to me, and ultimately of my own receptive responses to it. I am beginning to observe the multigenerational aspects of this unspoken legacy I inherited, pretty much without perceiving it consciously as it transpired. In my family, there is now an implicit imperative to plan and participate in the transmissions of end-of-life wishes and details. Perhaps you're concluding that something similar will be desirable for your own family and friends.

REFLECTING ON THESE REFLECTIONS

In this chapter, I'll be doing some more reflecting, or "thinking out loud" on paper. In addition to my surmises springing from my maternal grandfather's death, I'll use chapter 11 as a kind of "catch all" to help me reflect on and wrap up some of the various thoughts, stories, and exercises that are floating rather constantly in my mind while I'm still writing—as I wake up in the morning, go for a long walk, cook, or just "do nothing." These reflections are my con-stant partners now that the book is so close to being finished, and yet there's still a great deal of information it seems important to include.

REFLECTING ON LEGACY: A STORY

I live across the street from Lincoln Center. One particular evening when I felt as though there was nothing left in me to write, I carefully cleared my desk, shut down the computer, and walked over to the David Geffen Hall box office to get a ticket for that evening's concert. You'll probably find this true story as unlikely as I did as it unfolded, but here it is.

The concert started early, at 7:30 p.m., and a lot of the attendees were really dressed up. The women were wearing long, fancy dresses with very high heels, and the men were in suits with ties, despite the fact that these days New York City concertgoers are typically relaxed in their attire, in virtually all circumstances. This very fancy attire was unusual enough that it caught my attention. The first concert piece was the forty-minute Brahms Concerto in D Major for Violin and Orchestra, and while it was splendid, by itself it did nothing to help me understand this unusually formally dressed crowd.

After the intermission, however, it became clear why so many people were dressed to the nines. A brief speech explained to the audience that tonight was an annual special event. It was special because we were celebrating the many retired members of the New York Philharmonic Orchestra—particularly those who were in the audience at the concert—and there was going to be a private party, held in their honor, after the last two pieces had been performed.

That's interesting enough, I suppose, but you're likely to be wondering, "What does that have to do with this book?" Specifically, how does it relate to this chapter on reflections, which follows two chapters in which we've been learning about and considering creating Legacy Documents of our own, and then one chapter about obstacles to successful communications?

It turned out that two members of the orchestra were being specially honored since they were officially retiring on this very night, after thirty-seven years each of performing in the orchestra. Each of them had prepared remarks to present to the audience. Still wondering about the connection? Read on as I tell you a bit of what each of these musicians said, and I expect it will become more evident.

Charles Rex, violin, spoke first. He was articulate. He was retiring from his thirty-seven-year tenure with the New York Philharmonic and the Shirley Bacot Shamel Chair. He was going on to teach music history and violin at a small college in Connecticut. As he concluded his remarks, he specifically noted: "the living *legacy* of a great musical tradition? That's the New York Philharmonic!"

Further, almost as if they had coordinated their remarks with each other, and also pertinent to this book, Dawn Hannay, viola, now a brand-new retiree and the former chairperson of the Orchestra Committee, pronounced, "Life is short and (for me) the arts are what make it human." She left that *legacy* of her own for each of us in the audience—to appreciate, and perhaps also to reflect upon.

I hope this clarifies my own reflections on the "coincidence" this concert signified for me. In these two particular situations, it is *music that functions as the shape of beauty that is able to move the gloom away from frequently oppressive qualities of daily life,* for these musicians, and for many others. The expression of this belief puts Keats's words into sharper focus for me, and I hope equally so for you. This musical beauty certainly lifted my spirit.

I know neither of these musicians personally, but I reflect on the way that each of them is creating a particular legacy derived from their love of music specifically and appreciation of the arts in general. Each of them expressed their desire to continue to include music and the arts in their future life plans, and further, to let this love of music serve as a legacy. In each of these instances, a musician has proffered a sort of "Legacy Document" that is neither verbal nor written. Their Legacy Documents comprise the beauty of both their individual music and the entire New York Philharmonic. Brought to your attention, these stories reflect expanding the options that are open to you as well, especially if you are considering creating some sort of personally appropriate Legacy Document.

A WRY, EVEN FUNNY, REFLECTION, IN RETROSPECT

Hindsight is said to be 20/20, and in this case, it might have been. My parents and I had discussed what seemed at the time to be absolutely everything I'd need to know in order to help them trust that their articulated end-of-life thoughts covered all eventualities and would be carried out as they had described. I knew all the pertinent facts, and I had resources to contact for any questions that might arise.

I recognize that my situation deviated from the majority of families at the time in some particular ways because of the geography of our lives. My folks lived in Brooklyn, New York, my mother's surgery was in Manhattan, and I drove in from my home in Westport, Connecticut, to be with my mother, before and after her surgery. The pertinent issue here, however, is clothing.

I was wearing jeans and a T-shirt when I picked up my mother and drove her to the hospital, and I had brought with me another shirt or two. I was in nice but casual clothing, entirely appropriate for early June on the East Coast. I was staying at the home of a girlfriend, Melanie, who lived only a couple of blocks from the hospital where my mother was being treated. I knew I could wash and wear again whatever I'd brought with me.

I was, in fact, totally unprepared with anything like the appropriate clothing I needed after my mother died postoperatively; I had, of course, anticipated and prepared for her uncomplicated recovery. Never, in any of my discussions with my mom, from the first telephone call when she and my father told me all the details of their wishes and the accompanying information, had any of us given any thought to *clothing*. Yet, in the sudden chaos caused by her death, it became obvious that the omission of an "advance directive" for funeral attire was absolutely our only oversight.

What I needed urgently was a black dress, shoes, pocketbook, and so on, to wear at my mother's funeral. As Initiators, my parents had been explicit and thorough in telling me of everything that was needed for a funeral when the time came—except my own need for having handy, appropriate black mourner's garb. This had never been given a single thought by any of us. That's why I mention it now. Reflecting on the situation, I'm not sure how it could have been anticipated any differently—although I have recently heard that the British royal family travels with dark suits (and ties for the men) "just in case." But hearing this part of my story may turn out to be useful for others, particularly now, when families so rarely live close to one another, seldom even in the same "village."

We were lucky in many ways, my daughters, my father, and I. We responded exactly as Mother had wanted to this unanticipated outcome of hip replacement surgery, but this one ludicrous *sartorial* aspect stands out for me.

You're curious about how we dealt with it? A dear friend of mine, and mother of two of my daughters' closest friends, drove her children over to spend the night at our Westport house as soon as the girls called to tell them what had happened. Without any questions, she packed for me a black dress of hers, a pair of black shoes, a large black pocketbook (with two hankies in it), and some other useful things. She never discussed this trivia, only handing the bag with the clothing in it to my elder daughter, saying, "Your mom will need this. Take it with you to the city and be sure to give it to her tomorrow morning."

When I received the bag that next, harrowing morning, I looked inside and for a moment could do nothing except laugh out loud (and then cry). Everything I needed was there for me. Another wonderful gift. The wry humor in it never fails to warrant some mention when I talk about this anomalous

Listener aspect of my discussion about end-of-life matters. I reflect on it often, usually without knowing whether to actually mention it in public, or keep the story hidden. I admit that speaking about it usually wins out.

A Postscript

Twice now, subsequent to my teaching and leading workshops on end-of-life matters and their successful communication, I have been told that my comments about "*proper clothing just in case*" have been taken to heart, tucked away with a smile—just in case—and proven useful. It's funny, the things that we remember!

Michaela lived in New Hampshire with her husband and two high school–age children. She had readily agreed to be Listener for the end-of-life matters of both of her parents, even though she had two younger (also adult) siblings. Her folks, now in their early nineties and spry, still lived in the original family home in the country on the outskirts of Richmond, Virginia. Visits home meant hosting a few barbeques so Michaela's folks could entertain neighbors and other friends, doing some deep housecleaning for them, dog walking, and enjoying a generally relaxed week. In fact, it had been several years since they'd taken a drive into Richmond, even to see a movie.

Michaela, however, had participated in one of my lectures and chuckled about how I'd ultimately needed appropriate clothing for my mom's funeral, but had never thought to bring clothing like that with me, even just as a ludicrous precaution. As she prepared her family for their next visit to Virginia to be with her parents, she packed an entire set of clothing that they would either never need to wear during their visit or that she could pull out if indeed "something happened." She did this covertly, knowing she'd be ridiculed if nothing untoward happened and her family found out about her emergency stash—*of funeral clothes.*

Well, "happen" something did! On the second morning of their visit, Michaela's dad didn't feel quite right after breakfast. She drove him to his doctor's office while Mom and the rest of the family hung out at the house, doing chores. The doctor advised them to go immediately to the hospital in town, which they did, not even stopping to call home. Tests were run, and a decision had to be made about having or refusing a surgical procedure, a stent. "*No extraordinary measures*" had been the request of both parents, and Michaela had agreed to follow that directive. But a stent? Her understanding was that it was an easy enough procedure to perform without problems and would end up being very successful. Dad nodded affirmatively to the suggestion, and he was wheeled to the operating room without Michaela having to figure out for him if it was an ordinary or extraordinary procedure.

Relieved, she sat in the waiting room and called her mom and the rest of the family at the house. She urged them to come to the hospital and be there together when they'd be able to see him. They all were there with her within thirty minutes. Ten minutes after they'd gotten there and settled in for a wait, the cardiologist came to see them, looking very somber. Things had not gone as well as expected. Dad had had a heart attack during the procedure, and the odds were no longer in his favor.

It became a long and anxiety-filled wait for the ultimate outcome, which had been unanticipated and was very sad. Dad was in the intensive care unit, in a coma, and not expected to rally. Mom was permitted to visit him and talked to him without knowing if any of what she said got through to him. She felt better, however, for the opportunity. Michaela also got to visit with him and say how much she loved him, while her husband alerted her siblings and their families by cell phone, and travel plans were set in motion for them.

Michaela's dad died early that evening, and funeral plans were made per his wishes. Later that night, after things had quieted down a bit, and they were getting ready for bed, Michaela's husband offered to run into Richmond the next morning and see what sort of clothing he could find for all of them. Shaking her head, Michaela very quietly told her immediate family how she'd heard this weird story from me, and that when she'd packed, she remembered to include the clothing they'd all need—just in case. It gave them all a laugh, too.

I'm Not Being Sexist; Clothing's Important for Male Listeners, Too

John and his widowed father lived less than an hour's drive from one another, and talked pretty much daily. Dad had been involved with aspects of early childhood education at Stanford University until he retired, and kept in touch regularly with colleagues. John, who was thirty-four, had a responsible position at a tech startup in Silicon Valley. John was preparing to move the very next day to Palo Alto, where his dad lived. His current home was entirely packed up for the move, and he planned to stay at a hotel that evening.

John received an atypical telephone call at his office around 2:00 p.m. from one of his dad's friends who was concerned because he was supposed to meet John's dad for lunch at 1:00 p.m. and was still waiting for him to show up. There was no answer to the telephone in Dad's apartment. The friend hoped John could tell him what to do. John told him to stay put in case his father showed up and to call if he did, but John had keys and was going over to his dad's place immediately.

Dad was sitting slumped over in a chair, barely conscious when John walked in, and in a cold sweat from intense pain that he thought was abdominal. John immediately called an ambulance and got emergency medical care. His dad died in the late afternoon. In a state of complete shock and grief, but knowing all the end-of-life wishes his father had expressed, John was able to set up a funeral for the next day congruent with their religious preferences. After the arrangements had been finalized, it occurred to John that his clothing was all packed and would be impossible to find. He had no clothing at the hotel but the T-shirt and jeans he was wearing, and a clean set of underwear. *What was he going to do?*

One of his coworkers offered to lend him some khakis, a proper shirt, tie, and sports jacket, and so John got through the funeral looking, as he put it, *"like a mensch."* Are these two experiences, and mine, going to start a new trend, namely, keep dark clothing handy when traveling to be with someone you know or care about who is hospitalized? I hardly think so! But forewarned remains forearmed, as my mother used to say.

EXERCISE: REFLECTIONS, FOR INITIATORS, AND FOR LISTENERS

Let's begin this short, provocative writing exercise with an awareness of the two perspectives I've highlighted throughout *Your End of Life Matters*, those of Initiators and Listeners.

I suggest that you plan to take between ten and twenty minutes to reflect on the writing prompt I will give you, and then do a mental review of what you've been reading and thinking about in our work together. The writing prompt is the same for both Initiators and Listeners, although their perspectives on it will be different.

Here's the writing prompt: *"I wonder . . ."*

Those of you who identify with the Initiators will want primarily to consider the information you're transmitting to your Listener(s). You might reflect on whether you've left any things or people out or have been so focused on your own needs and feelings that you've overlooked anything you'd want to include. One very brief example: "I wonder what it's like to be on the receiving end of this request. Is there some additional way I can make my appreciation clear that might be helpful? Is there something about this that I should ask to bring up for us to discuss further?"

In contrast, those of you who identify with the Listener(s) of a communication will be asking yourself what you've been quiet about, failed to bring into the open, or failed to pursue with questions. Here's a beginning set of possible Listener reflections: "I wonder if I've been sensitive enough to how my sibling(s) will feel to have been left out from this communication. Will they feel hurt? Might they be angry at me? What can I do to help us revise what we're planning to do?"

The last step in this exercise is to take a deep breath, reflect on what you've written, and see if you have fully responded to the writing prompt. Note in your journal the way you feel about the prompt and the response it evoked. With that completed, at least for the time being, you've finished your work with this particular writing prompt.

ONE FURTHER PERSONAL REFLECTION

There have been times when I've found it difficult to keep myself immersed in writing the manuscript that has become this book. It's been demanding in a way that writing no other book has been for me. That's because there are many aspects of this book, some articulated here in print, others not, that have a direct, inescapable connection with dying and death. That's material many people resist, want nothing to do with, avoid considering, and certainly don't want to see on their night table. Even the people who are interested in reading or talking about dying and death acknowledge that it's difficult material, and they don't usually immerse themselves in it for long spans of time.

I do not allow myself the luxury *cum* fantasy of denying the reality of death, the ultimate ending to every life that begins. Whether I like it or not, I cannot deny knowing that I am part of "everyone" in the short sentence: Everyone dies. I understand that we absolutely never know what the number or quality will be of the days that lie ahead of each of us. There are no promises of longevity or health or even of things necessarily seeming to work out in ways that are "fair"! Life begins, we cut teeth, learn to walk and talk, have preferences of many kinds and experiences, and then—boom—suddenly life ends. Emily Dickinson wrote about the rapidity of the experience, noting, "Old age comes on suddenly, and not gradually as is thought." Thinking it comes on gradually is, I'm afraid, part of our denial that old age (or poor health or unhappiness or being unduly vulnerable) will come on at all—*for me*.

With all that said, I continue to maintain that this is not a book about death! What it is in fact is a book about communication. The communications we focus on throughout this volume do have something to do with the reality of death because we are working out how best to communicate information about our own end-of-life data and wishes. This "ending of life" is related to the process of dying and, yes, dying is followed by death. The activity we focus on, however, throughout the introduction and twelve chapters that make up the bulk of the text remains *communication*. The exercises and stories are focused on the various steps you can take to think about personal

General, Effective Methods of Communication

A list follows of some of the principal methods of communication you see in these chapters. Communication is our focus, and the material I am teaching is primarily about techniques of successful communication, highlighted with many illustrative stories and exercises. The methods pertain to successful communication in general, not exclusively to that having to do with your end-of-life matters.

- Speak for yourself; use *I* not *you* to start a conversation.
- Listen carefully and ask questions when anything is unclear. When in doubt, repeat what you think you've heard and check it out.
- Use only *good* humor when you're trying to be funny or to make a point; it's a joining agent.
- Avoid sarcasm; it can easily destroy goodwill.
- Keep in mind that trust is a highly desirable quality for all participants in a successful conversation; agreement may follow, but trust is a primary essential.
- Be flexible; there's often more than just one "right way."
- Be clear! Ask for what you want, and be sure that what you want is understood by the person (people) you're addressing.

aspects of yourself, first how to think about and identify your end-of-life matters, and then how to effectively communicate these matters to an accepting, appropriate person who will promise to carry them out. I recognize that I could just as easily have used these principles of communication to help you deal with some other topic, as I often do in my family therapy practice. But this is the topic that I believe is most timely, as well as one with which I have had unique, firsthand experience.

ONE FURTHER KEY QUESTION TO ADDRESS

Clearly, I'm my mother's daughter, and the need for people to think about, and then talk about, their end-of-life matters seems to me, as it did for her, to be important, even desirable. As you realize, I know personally the benefits of being first a Listener and then an Initiator. In addition, as I worked both at Mt. Sinai Hospital in New York City, and in my therapy practice in the city and in Westport, Connecticut, the need for someone to speak out about why and how to talk about end-of-life matters was unavoidably persistent. So I decided to tackle it.

Despite the importance here of the topics related to end-of-life matters, at its core *this is a book about successful* **communication**. *This book is neither about dying nor death. Rather, it is a guide to communicating or listening to end-of-life matters including pertinent details and wishes, often through conversations.*

As we progress now to chapter 12, we are finally preparing to answer **When?**, our sixth and last key question. Throughout the book, I've urged you to be thoughtful and to consciously communicate, with the greatest possible clarity, your end-of-life wishes successfully as an Initiator, or to receive and agree to carry them out as a Listener, or perhaps both in some sequence (as I was).

12

Face the Ultimate Question: When?

If not now, when?

—Hillel (the Elder), Early Jewish Sage, Born in Babylon
(ca. 110 BCE–10 CE)

$\mathscr{I}$n the lexicon of conversations about end-of-life matters, Initiators are almost always the people who first ask themselves each of our six key questions, of which **When?** is the last. By the time an Initiator is reading about and preparing to consider **When?** (to schedule this communication), she or he will have read all the way through this book, or completed a book group or its therapeutic equivalent, and will have finished doing the preparatory work for a conversation or other kind of communication about end-of-life matters. It's also the job of Initiators to organize, plan, and then *initiate* this conversation. What's more, Initiators are the people who need to acknowledge the fact that it is not too late to begin this communication process. As Rilke counseled poets, people are neither too old nor too young to move forward. Applying this thought to our work, I'd say that no matter what your age is, *when you are ready* is the right time to plan and have a worthwhile communication about various end-of-life matters, including both data and wishes.

Many readers will have determined that initiating is not their task at this particular point in time. Rather, they are poised to help someone else express their own end-of-life needs and wishes. It is beneficial to experience being on both sides of this conversation, and I hope you will do so in time, but the initial decision of where to begin is entirely in the heart and hands of each individual reader. For the purposes of this last chapter, the primary focus will often be on the Initiator's responsibilities as the time for beginning the communication about end-of-life matters is identified.

An Initiator's Progress

By the time we are getting ready to answer this ultimate question, **When?**, Initiators, who may be at any age or stage of life, have already covered a lot of ground. They have:

- understood the nature and benefits of an end-of-life conversation by hearing relevant stories and participating in thinking and writing exercises on the topic;
- identified a Listener;
- carefully planned the information to be shared with the Listener;
- thought through why it's important and perhaps also timely to have this conversation;
- figured out how and where to hold the conversation;
- learned about and considered creating a Legacy Document (or not); and
- reached readiness to initiate their conversation in the near future. **When?** is their only key question remaining to be answered.

At the risk of saying the obvious, as Initiator, you are the one who has thought through and made the many decisions about all the aspects of your end-of-life communication so far. You've devised answers to five of the six key questions—**Who?**, **What?**, **Why?**, **How?**, and **Where?**—that focus the content you've decided to include in the discussion of your end-of-life matters. You've considered and included any other relevant information to this point. Ultimately, however, one last question must enter the picture regarding your conversation, and be answered: **When?**

It would seem, at first, that this is a question that's quite easy to answer: "*The sooner the better!*" (Or, as Hillel would be apt to respond to **When?**: "Now!") You are probably going to discover that when you are attempting to schedule a person-to-person meeting of any sort (either in person or via Skype, or even just by telephone), agreeing on the timing of your meeting can become more difficult than you'd hoped or anticipated.

It's likely that you, the Initiator, will plan to invite your Listener(s) to meet you and join in this conversation at a time and place of your choice. If they say yes, your potential problems are over. When that isn't the case, you're at a juncture where you'll do best if you actually cede control to a certain extent. The reality is that your Listener(s), the person or people who make up your **Who?**, will be the one(s) whose calendar, willingness, and ability to talk with you will primarily govern the answer to **When?**

Most Initiators can accept this as a given. If, on the other hand, letting your Listener(s) decide **When?** you will be able to talk together has become troubling to you, you may need to go back to the drawing board and consider developing a written communication or, an even more drastic change, you may decide to reconsider your choice of Listener(s).

When the time comes to actually arrange a conversation, you'll need to face and accept the reality of scheduling difficulties as graciously and patiently as possible. At the same time, you'll want to do your best to discern avoidance as differentiated from actual, valid commitments that make it impossible to meet when you've suggested, or as soon as you'd like. You'll probably remember that this capacity to adjust is what Janet was faced with and managed to do, very flexibly, when the unanticipated pregnancy announcement of son Larry and his wife, Susan, preempted her own conversation plans. (We learned about this story in the **Where?** section of chapter 7.)

For those Initiators who have decided to emulate my parents' approach, to make a single telephone call to a Listener, without any advance preparation regarding either time or topic—go for it. That certainly makes it unlikely that you'll be blocked from proceeding by avoidant behaviors on the part of your Listener(s).

You may also want to suggest setting up a follow-up telephone call (or a subsequent face-to-face meeting) in case there are questions or thoughts that come up after the initial communication is over. Question six (**When?**) can certainly crop up more than once. Think about this: When and how will you want to schedule a follow-up meeting if one is wanted?

Whatever you do, be respectful. You're asking something of your Listener(s) that may not be immediately possible to arrange. Busy schedules can indeed be tricky to negotiate.

A jammed calendar, however, is sometimes used as an excuse when a Listener is uncomfortable with what he or she thinks is going to be discussed. A direct question from the Initiator might include, "I'd really prefer to work this out with **you**. But if scheduling is going to continue to be this hard for us, would you prefer for me to stop trying to include you in this conversation?"

I want to be very clear. In a situation like this, a practical Initiator will be thinking ahead about who could be his or her plan B, replacement Listener. This step should only be in the thinking stage and never posited as a threat. It isn't something to consider talking about while you're still negotiating with your first choice for Listener. Threatening isn't something an Initiator would ever benefit from doing.

DRAWBACKS TO NOT REVISITING
CONVERSATIONS: A STORY

It's important to remind ourselves that, in many instances, we don't get second chances for our conversation to take place. What comes to mind first when you hear those words is that the people deciding to initiate this conversation are frequently at what appears to be a final life stage, from either illness or advanced age. However, sometimes there are younger candidates for a conversation, like Lenny and Audrey, whose story follows, who might miss out on a second chance because they were in no hurry, believing they'd get to plan their conversation "whenever."

At the time of their thirtieth wedding anniversary, Lenny and Audrey were in their early fifties, in good health, and working full-time. He was a physician, she a teacher. They had two sons, each in his mid-twenties. After decades of thinking about having end-of-life conversations, but doing nothing productive, now seemed like a sensible time for them to actually discuss their end-of-life thoughts and wishes, first with each other, and then with their sons as well. The couple reviewed their notes on what to include, planned their talk, and called the boys to find a good time for a conversation. The boys agreed to meet with their parents, and later that year, they were able to have a thorough, onetime conversation that seemed satisfying to all of them.

Fast-forward twenty-five years. Both sons are married now, and one has children. Lenny and Audrey have been married fifty-five years at this point, are in their late seventies, and no longer work. Lenny enjoys playing golf and bowling, but one day he pulls some muscles, which go into spasm, and walking becomes seriously painful. Driving soon becomes impossible for him, and since he's never liked being the passenger, he's stuck at home quite a lot.

Audrey, on the other hand, seems physically pretty much as she's always been, but Lenny and she both recognize that she has begun forgetting things. She's no longer an entirely reliable reporter of how things are going in the household. Neither they nor their sons are able to know if this is normal for her age or something to worry about, and they're in a wait-and-see mode, which seems okay, short term. Shortly after Lenny could no longer manage getting around without help, he becomes quite sick, within weeks. He has developed a pattern of internal bleeding episodes that seem to come and go. Stubborn, he does not want to be hospitalized. What's the family (read: his sons, their Listeners) to do? No one knows if Lenny should be allowed to make his own medical decisions at this point. It's too late now to go back five or ten years to revisit the carefully thought-through original conversation which, in their case, left one spouse in decision-making control if the other wasn't able to be. That seems possibly dangerous, at least unrealistic, with both partners now compromised.

Our question in this chapter is **When?**. When do you have your first communication about end-of-life matters, and when is it a good idea to have one or more follow-up conversations? Lenny and Audrey's radically changed situation, twenty-five years after their first conversation, demonstrates that in circumstances like these, with an initial conversation happening before an Initiator's mid-to-late sixties, the first conversation may not always suffice. Is it possible, generally speaking, for the initial conversation to remain valid forever? Not highly likely, I'm sorry to report.

When communication is initiated by an adult of any age in a stage of life that appears unlikely to change very much in the future, one conversation may indeed suffice. If, however, the sixty-year-old Initiator is single and has just started a new graduate school program, it would probably be wise to review the plans annually for the next decade or so, while this Initiator's lifestyle evolves. It's probably a wise idea for the Initiator to figure this out for herself or himself in the early stages of planning to communicate end-of-life matters.

Is there a benefit to briefly and comfortably revisiting end-of-life conversations after five, ten, or twenty years, or perhaps at all of those times? These answers are best left to each individual Initiator and each situation. I raise the questions specifically so that you can give thought to what would be best for you and consciously plan to act according to what you recognize is in your best interest.

WHY NOT?—A STORY

Louise, a married woman in her mid-fifties, had participated in a group I facilitated in Connecticut and became well informed about end-of-life matters, the relevant paperwork, and conversations. She felt young enough, however, to be in no hurry to initiate talking with her husband initially. Even so, her husband, Tom, three years younger than she, was fifty-four when he began to exhibit behaviors she considered "atypical for him." He would get angry in ways that seemed irrational to her and that were also out of character for him. He'd been a contractor, a union member, and always easygoing, cooperative, and well liked, but she described him as having become quick to anger, very easily frustrated by ordinary changes in work orders and such, for several months before she asked to meet privately with me. To make matters even more confusing, Tom was misplacing things like his set of car or house keys, the newspaper, or his water glass, and blaming her for moving them. He was also consuming more alcohol than usual. Louise was becoming worried about her own judgment, and that's ultimately what provoked her to call me for the consult.

Following an additional consultation with her internist (who had a sub-specialty in geriatrics), we were able to conclude that the problem Louise had was not due to an early dementia causing issues with her own memory, but with stress-induced forgetfulness. The fact was that some of the symptoms her husband was showing pointed to the possibility that he was the one who had signs of early-onset dementia, and she was frightened as well as worried.

Louise needed to have a conversation about end-of-life matters and there was no longer time to wait to do that. Perhaps it could still be with Tom first, but more likely she was going to have to choose someone for a follow-up whom they both felt close to and trusted. She organized the conversation herself, for both of them, guessing as best she could what Tom would want their Listener to know. The communication she began to prepare focused on the matters like important end-of-life needs, thoughts, or decisions they'd have plus any details related to them. For Louise, having Tom abruptly face an illness that looked serious, radically affected her own present life. What's more, her (their) ability to deal with the future was undergoing a stunning, profound change.

Tom had been the Listener Louise would have had in mind for her own wishes. Now, abruptly, not only did she no longer have an obvious Listener of her own, Louise felt she had to initiate an entirely different conversation with Tom, one really about himself, not both of them. It was imperative, as she put it, to talk together "before it got too late for this kind of talking."

Louise was right. **When?** was no longer a casual question for her, to be thought about and answered sometime after she'd entered her sixties. **When?** had become a question with a burning need to be answered immediately. Urgently, she felt. She was overwhelmed.

Even so, Louise thought through her individual wishes and needs, de-tailed her banking and legal paperwork, and made two appointments before approaching Tom. The first was with her attorney. The second was a coffee date with her younger brother and sister, clarifying for all three what she felt comprised the relevant details for herself. With these discussions behind her, she scheduled an appointment for Tom and herself with their internist, hop-ing this would work out well for each of them.

The lesson we take from Louise's story is that, in real life, things don't always develop the way we've been expecting them to. In those instances, you need to amend accordingly the **When?** timeline for your conversations. Go ahead and change your timeline, but don't let that changing put off for too long the start of your actual conversation.

EXERCISE: GETTING TO WHEN?

Refer to your journal as you consider the following questions, forming a short review:

1. Have you done all the exercises throughout the book that you thought would be helpful in preparing your thoughts for this discussion?
2. Are there any exercises you want to return to now and review? Any notes in your journal that might warrant looking back at?
3. Is there anything else you need to help you take this next step? If so, what is it, and how will you get what you need? Keep journaling every day, until you're ready and able to move beyond the stuck place, even if that means it'll be slightly longer before you can get started with your actual conversation.
4. Prepare notes and a script that you can use just in case you might feel you're losing focus during the conversation.
5. When is the right time for you to initiate this discussion? *"Now!"* is indeed what I hope will finally be your answer to **When?**.

The very last step has to do exclusively with appreciating and enjoying the rest of your life. Let that be your biggest challenge, and may you meet it daily with gratitude, satisfaction, and pleasure! It's your life, no one else's. I hope you'll have time and energy to choose to live it fully, acknowledging some good in every day you have. Starting When? Now, of course!

Appendix A

A Guide for Book Groups

If you would like to work in the company of a book group, either as you read this book or as a follow-up after you've finished reading it, the first task is to identify your group members. It's common for people to set up a "pre–book group" meeting at which non-content-related topics are discussed as follows:

PRE–BOOK GROUP ORGANIZATIONAL MEETING

1. Will you limit the size of the group to a maximum? (Eight members is usually a good maximum for these groups. This allows enough time for all members to have a chance to talk at each meeting, if they want to.)
2. Where will you meet? Do you prefer a community meeting room, at a local library, for example? If so, who will take responsibility for reserving the space? What are your requirements for the space? If you prefer to meet at member homes, will your meetings rotate among homes or be in just one place?
3. How frequently do you want to meet? You might choose weekly, monthly, or something in between.
4. How long should your meetings last? Groups sometimes build in a half-hour first for socializing and catching up before the actual book discussion is set to begin. In most groups, the *book discussion* part lasts for an hour.

5. Will snacks of some sort be served? Beverages? Or just "bring your own water"? If you want snacks and/or beverages, who will coordinate these for each meeting?

6. Are members responsible to have read the whole book before the group starts, or to read one chapter at a time before each meeting? Should members not come to a meeting if they haven't read the relevant material, or is it okay to come and just "wing it"? Every group has its own feelings about this; it's helpful if you can decide in advance of your first content-related meeting which option will work best for your group. We *suggest* the particular chapters to read in advance of each meeting as outlined.

7. Encourage members to use a journal of some sort, not only as they work through the exercises in the book but also to bring to the group for making notes or following additional writing prompts.

8. Will you have the same *leader* throughout the series of meetings, or do you prefer to set up a rotation of some sort?

9. Set the schedule for your book group, checking members' calendars to be sure you've cleared holidays and other dates that might reduce attendance in a particular week.

10. Be sure to get e-mail addresses of all members and agree that any and all book group–related information will be communicated by e-mail.

11. Do you have any interest in inviting the author to come and speak to your group or to a larger group (library, senior center, organization, school, bookstore, etc.) in your community? If so, who will assume responsibility for querying the author (at ziffaf@gmail.com)?

LEADING BOOK GROUP DISCUSSIONS, MEETINGS ONE THROUGH ELEVEN

Meeting One

Suggestion: Members will have read at least the introduction and chapter 1.

Regardless of whether all members of the book group already know one another fairly well or are strangers, the leader starts this first group with a brief (maximum three minutes) introduction of herself or himself and *the reason(s) for her or his interest in this discussion group* focused on *Your End of Life Matters*. What made reading the book with a group preferable to reading the book on your own? After the leader comments, each member takes a turn, exchanging the same sort of introductory information.

Here are some questions to reflect on for the balance of this first meeting:

- You've read Anne's introduction to the book and the first chapter. If you were she, how do you think you would have felt getting that telephone call from your own parents?
- Do you think you would make an important telephone call like that?
- How do you feel about considering the call (or its contents) "the gift of a lifetime"? At this point, do you think you would value it that way or prefer something else as your "gift of a lifetime"?

Meeting Two

Our topic this week focuses on *stories*, based on having read chapter 2. *Your End of Life Matters: How to Talk With Family and Friends* is a book that begins with a story, not a "once upon a time" story, but a taboo-breaking story that Anne, the author, has been touched by, thought about, and followed through on by talking, teaching, and writing about. This is a story that she believes is valuable for people outside of her own family to hear, to think about, and perhaps to use to spark behaviors of their own.

- Does your family have any stories that are unique and representative of you in this way? What are they?
- If not, what comes close to being an important family behavior or memory, transmitted through at least one other generation, the way this story has been?
- Do you have any particular feelings, pro or con, about Anne's story and her use of it?

Let's consider how many group members are curious about experiencing an end-of-life matters conversation of their own inside their family.

- Which group members are at a stage of life where they'd be comfortable as an Initiator? Who as a Listener?
- If you are currently better suited to be a Listener, do you think you will have to prompt a particular family member or friend to have this conversation? How might you feel about listening to his or her needs and wishes? Is this a reasonable position for you to be in, or would you have to admit you couldn't take on that responsibility? How would you say so, if that were the case?

Anne suggests that humor may help in a conversation on such a serious topic.

- How do you respond to jokes about aging or the end of life?
- Would you be comfortable using humor in your conversation?

Leader: Encourage members to bring in jokes, cartoons, or quips to share at the next meeting.

Meeting Three

Suggestion: Members will have read chapter 3.

Before moving into today's topic, share humorous items members have brought. Discuss how such items might be used in developing the conversation, either as a Listener or as an Initiator.

In chapter 3, Anne introduces the topic of a family's conversation history.

- What was the conversation history in your own family when you were growing up? What about in your family as an adult?

Have you ever thought of creating a bucket list of your own? Write one together as a group and then spend five to ten minutes creating your own personal list. List as many items as you can think of; when you've run out of ideas, identify the one that is most important to you, and number the others in decreasing order of importance. Discuss how you might set about making the most important item happen.

Anne poses six key questions to be considered when planning a conversation about end-of-life matters and wishes: **Who?**, **What?**, **Why?**, **How?**, **Where?**, and **When?**. She suggests **Who?** is the first question to consider.

- Do you agree with that choice? If not, which question would you start with? Discuss the pros and cons of beginning with **Who?** versus with one of the other questions.

Meeting Four

In chapter 4, Anne guides readers to think as an Initiator and focus on **Who?** to ask to be the Listener to their conversation. Is that a hard or easy task for you? It's certainly one in which an Initiator, of any age, will feel vulnerable, an emotion that is often difficult to express.

Anne writes that, at some point, her agent insisted she step out of her early role of Listener and involve herself actively as an Initiator before writing the rest of the book. This would allow her to more completely understand the considerations, tensions, and vulnerabilities involved for Initiators.

- What do *you* think about that? Is it better for the author of a "how-to" book to be personally experienced with the tasks, or do you think theoretical knowledge is sufficient to make an author an expert?
- If you had been the author in Anne's place, how might you have responded to your agent's recommendation?

In focusing on **Who?** first, Anne emphasizes the importance of choosing a Listener who can and will respect and carry out your wishes.

- Who would *you* think to choose as Listener if you were the one initiating a conversation (at any age) about end-of-life matters? What might provoke you to think you'd like to ask this person or people to become your Listener(s)?
- Do you think you need to have a "plan-B" Listener in mind, just in case?
- Do you think you'd like to also have a health-care practitioner as your Listener? If so, do you have someone in mind? (Discussion—who, why, any rule-outs?) Are you ready to make the telephone call to his or her office? If not, what would help you get there?

Meeting Five

The topic in chapter 5 is **What?**, and its content is much more concrete and less emotion producing than that of many of the earlier chapters.

- Did you find this material easier to work with? Why or why not?

For some people, putting together all this information is really emotionally overwhelming, and so it's very difficult to manage. For others, it's "just papers" and no big deal to assemble.

- Where do you think you fit in with the material that belongs as the **What?** for this conversation? Can you easily assemble it in your cell phone or computer for your Listener? Does it represent an overwhelming mass of papers and other data?

How's your health? Group members may be uncomfortable talking about this topic, so offer the option of writing responses, rather than a verbal go-around.

- Give some thought to what you want to reveal to your Listener about the status of your own health and how best to do that, particularly if there are issues to discuss that might come as a surprise. Make some notes, and plan what you might be comfortable saying.
- Would you want to be using a script or notes of some kind when the time comes to have this part of your conversation? Discuss the pros and cons of notes/scripts, acknowledging there's no one right answer, only a matter of preference.
- Are there any comments you'd like to make on the contrasts between the stories about Grandpa Louie and about Caroline? Does one move you more than the other? Which one, and why?
- The chapter about **What?** is written as a guide, not an absolute. What other items, if any, do you think should have been included? Do you think any items are unnecessary or inappropriate to share with your Listener?
- If you're considering having a conversation of your own at this point, are there topics beyond **Who?** and **What?** that you need to consider? If we follow Anne's sequence, **Why?** will be next. Would that be your choice, too, in this sequence of six key questions?

Meeting Six

Suggestion: Members will have read chapter 6.

- Can you see **Why?** this conversation might be valuable to you as Listener? To you as Initiator?
- Did having an end-of-life conversation occur to you before reading this book? If so, why did you consider it?
- When, during a lifetime, is it likely that thoughts of having this conversation may come up?
- Are you facing events or changes in your life that might make such a conversation particularly relevant now?
- What are the advantages of talking about your wishes with someone you know you can trust? Do you see any disadvantages?
- Is it possible that it's equally important for health-care professionals to choose to have a conversation of their own?

- How do you think and feel about Robert and Ethel's "Going Away Party for Old Friends"? Could you picture yourself having a party like that? Can you picture yourself attending an event like that?
- In contrast, think about Marjorie's story. How did you feel about it? Do you understand why she felt she had received *such a gift*? How might you have felt under similar circumstances?
- **Why?** have this conversation—as Jack and Margot determined, how could you not? What are your own thoughts about why to have an end-of-life conversation?
- How many members of the book group are seriously planning one of their own, at this point? How many not?

Meeting Seven

It's a challenge to consider **How?** and **Where?**, as chapter 7 guides you to do, but it's worth the effort, Anne writes. Do you agree? Once we add the answers to these two key questions, we have very little that stands in the way of having a fruitful end-of-life conversation.

- How do you feel about this?
- Do you know now what you're planning to do—to initiate a conversation of your own, to help someone else do that, or not to become involved with this topic of conversation at all? Where do you currently see yourself?
- Can you put yourself in Joe's place and imagine how scared you might feel if you were getting ready to ask someone to be your Listener? Wouldn't the distance of an e-mail really be protective, both for the Initiator and the Listener? (That was Joe's premise, which got shot down unceremoniously by Sue!) Do you have a better way to deal with any of the anxiety than by hiding it?
- As Initiator, how do you want to communicate your invitation to your Listener candidate?

Having dealt with four of the key questions, Anne suggests readers now focus on **Where?** to have their conversation.

- Do you think **Where?** should make a significant difference to your conversation?
- Do you think you could be flexible, as Janet was? How did you feel about that story? Did you identify with Janet or with her son and daughter-in-law?

Optional—Meetings Eight and Nine

Chapters 8 and 9 deal with a related, but optional topic, Legacy Documents. Talking about and developing Legacy Documents are challenging and interesting activities, but not essential to developing and communicating your end-of-life matters. Some groups will omit this topic entirely, some will work with the material in the sequence followed in the book, and still others will work with Legacy Documents *after* they have finished attending to specific issues of end-of-life conversations, during the final two meetings of the group session.

If your book group plans to discuss Legacy Documents, the most effective format would be for the group leader (or other members) to read salient portions of chapters 8 and 9 aloud during one session, with intermittent discussions. At the following meeting, group members would bring in their outlines or initial efforts for some form of Legacy Document. During either session, group members can discuss who it is that they hope will receive their Legacy Document, and when.

As always, if and when the material involved feels too personal for group process, those feelings should be respected, and the member is free to pass during discussion. Members should also feel free to ask questions, either about the process of creating a Legacy Document or the end product itself; if necessary review chapters 8 and 9.

Meeting Ten

Suggestion: This week's discussion centers on chapters 10 and 11.

Begin by assessing where each member is in terms of being involved in an end-of-life conversation.

- Do you see a value to yourself of having this conversation? If so, what do you still need to do to prepare for it? Is anything keeping you from completing your preparations?
- If you have decided that now is not the right time for you, what makes you think that? What might make you change your mind?
- During the discussion, are obstacles mentioned? Are any of these common to two or more members? Discuss possible ways to overcome the individual or common obstacles.
- How would you have felt if you'd been a guest at the holiday party Anne described? Can you imagine how uncomfortable she felt during the initial silence after she spoke? What might your thoughts have been if you were in her place?

- Do you have some thoughts and opinions about Sylvia's story and her behaviors?
- Do you have any thoughts about Sam's story?

This is the next to the last session working toward communicating end-of-life matters, including pertinent details and wishes.

- Do you have any thoughts about material that hasn't been included in this book-group discussion guide?
- Has your work on the conversation brought up memories or thoughts you'd like to reflect on with the group?

Meeting Eleven

When? is the sixth and final key question in the book (chapter 12), and also in this discussion guide. In the final week, we directly address the question of **When?** this end-of-life conversation will indeed be held (unless you remain reluctant or unwilling to initiate one). In the case of Lenny and Audrey, they held their conversation relatively early in their lives; as years passed, they failed to readdress their end-of-life matters, with difficult consequences.

- Are you likely to be in a similar situation? Do you think you could avoid it? Do you feel the need to plan more than one **When?**
- How do the circumstances in Louise and Tom's story affect your thinking about **When?** to initiate your own end-of-life conversation?
- Have you decided **When?** you will initiate an end-of-life conversation? What factors influenced your choice?

Anne encourages readers and Initiators to recognize that the answer to key question six, **When?**, is no longer exclusively, maybe not even primarily, the province of the Initiator. Scheduling and time and work considerations may be more or equally pressing for potential Listeners than they are for Initiators.

- Given your choice of Listener(s), what factors might interfere with successfully setting your time frame for a meeting? Do you have an alternate **When?** already in mind?
- Having chosen the **When?** for your end-of-life conversation, will you let it be a surprise, as Anne's parents did, or plan for it with the help of your Listener candidates? What do you think are the pros and cons of these choices?

Options for Ending the Book Group

Some groups continue to meet, at least one more time, to report to one another how the conversations went and whether further clarifying conversations will be needed. The group may meet also to assess whether members want to discuss creating a Legacy Document and, if so, how many additional meetings will be useful.

While formal reading-group outlines are time limited, groups discussing topics of this sort often continue indefinitely. Members find that the supportive aspects of the group can be both helpful and thought provoking. These decisions are up to members of each individual group. There is no one right or wrong way to conclude or continue.

I wish you stimulating reading and successful conversations, both in the book group and independently about your end-of-life matters.

Appendix B

A List of Euphemisms for Death or Dying

*M*any words are used to "beat around the bush" on the subjects of illness, death, and dying. A list of some of the more common euphemisms follows. These may give you something to smile about or help you expand your vocabulary for the desensitization exercise, "Make Yourself Comfortable," that is in chapter 2.

- Croaked
- Kicked the bucket
- Passed away
- Passed over to the other side
- If *something happens* to you/me . . .
- When the time comes . . .
- She/he is gone
- Sail into the sunset
- Meet your maker
- Joined their ancestors
- Face God
- The final exit (or final curtain)
- Pushing up daisies
- Put to sleep (typically about an animal)
- (Name) is at rest
- (Name) is at peace
- (Name) bit the dust
- (Name) is fading away
- (Name's) time has come
- (Name) didn't make it

References and Resources

Abraham, John. *How to Get the Death You Want: A Practical and Moral Guide*. Hinesburg, VT: Upper Access, 2017.

Allison, Jay, and Dan Gediman. *This I Believe: The Personal Philosophies of Remarkable Men and Women*. New York: Henry Holt, 2006.

Anthony, Mitch. *The New Retirementality: Planning Your Life and Living Your Dreams . . . at Any Age You Want*. Second edition. Chicago: Kaplan Publishing, 2006.

Arnold, Elizabeth. *Creating the Good Will: The Most Comprehensive Guide to Both the Financial and Emotional Sides of Passing on Your Legacy*. London: Portfolio, 2005.

Brewster, Victoria, and Julie Saeger Nierenberg. *Journey's End: Death, Dying, and the End of Life*. Bloomington, IN: Xlibris, 2017.

Caputo, Theresa. *Good Grief: Heal Your Soul, Honor Your Loved Ones, and Learn to Live Again*. New York: Atria Books, 2017.

Chast, Roz. *Can't We Talk about Something More Pleasant?: A Memoir*. New York: Bloomsbury USA, 2016.

Collins, Gail. "This Is What 80 Looks Like." *New York Times*, Sunday Review, March 22, 2014. https://nytimes/2mUR0vD.

Cooley, Martha. *Guesswork: A Reckoning with Loss*. New York: Catapult Publishing, 2017.

Crowe, Kelsey, and Emily McDowell. *There Is No Good Card for This: What to Say and Do When Life Is Scary, Awful, and Unfair to People You Love*. New York: HarperCollins, 2017.

Davidson, Sara. *The December Project: An Extraordinary Rabbi and a Skeptical Seeker Confront Life's Greatest Mystery*. New York: HarperCollins, 2015.

Egan, Kerry. *On Living*. New York: Penguin, 2016.

Erikson, Erik H., and Joan M. Erikson. *Life Cycle Completed*. New York: W.W. Norton, 1997.

Gawande, Atul. *Being Mortal: Medicine and What Matters in the End*. New York: Metropolitan Books, 2014.

Gerberg, Mort, ed. *Last Laughs: Cartoons about Aging, Retirement . . . and the Great Beyond.* New York: Scribner, 2007.

Grolnick, Simon. *The Work & Play of WINNICOTT.* Northvale, NJ: Jason Aronson, 1990.

I'm Dead, Now What? Important Information about My Belongings, Business Affairs, and Wishes [journal]. White Plains, NY: Peter Pauper Press, 2015.

Izzo, John B. *The Five Secrets You Must Discover before You Die.* San Francisco: Berrett-Koehler, 2008.

Levine, Robert A. *Aging Wisely: Strategies for Baby Boomers and Seniors.* Lanham, MD: Rowman & Littlefield, 2014.

Kabat-Zinn, Jon. *Mindfulness for Beginners: Reclaiming the Present Moment—and Your Life.* 2011. Reprint, Louisville, CO: Sounds True, 2016.

Kinsley, Michael. *Old Age: A Beginner's Guide.* New York: Tim Duggan Books, 2016.

Maslow, Abraham H. *Towards a Psychology of Being.* 1961. Reprint, Hoboken, NJ: John Wiley and Sons, 1998.

Mason, L. John. *Guide to Stress Reduction.* Revised edition. Berkeley, CA: Celestial Arts, 1986.

Riemer, Jack, and Nathaniel Stampfer, eds. *Ethical Wills & How to Prepare Them: A Guide to Sharing Your Values from Generation to Generation.* Second edition. Woodstock, VT: Jewish Lights, 2015.

Sandberg, Sheryl, and Adam Grant. *Option B: Facing Adversity, Building Resilience and Finding Joy.* New York: Knopf Doubleday, 2017.

Schaub, Bonney Gulino, and Richard Schaub. *Dante's Path: A Practical Approach to Achieving Inner Wisdom.* New York: Gotham Books, 2003.

Volandes, Angelo E. *The Conversation: A Revolutionary Plan for End-of-Life Care.* New York: Bloomsbury, 2015.

Weil, Andrew. *Healthy Aging: A Lifelong Guide to Your Physical and Spiritual Well-Being.* New York: Knopf Doubleday, 2005.

Williams, Mark, and Danny Penman. *Mindfulness: An Eight-Week Plan for Finding Peace in a Frantic World.* New York: Rodale Press, 2011.

Yalom, Irvin D. *Staring at the Sun: Overcoming the Terror of Death.* San Francisco: Jossey-Bass, 2008.

Ziff, Anne. "Leading Groups in a Senior Center." *GROUP, The Journal of the Eastern Group Psychotherapy Society* 40, no. 4 (2016): 343–56.

Acknowledgments

$\mathscr{I}$n the five years it took me to bring this manuscript from concept to completion as a book, many, many people stayed tuned in, talking me through the writing process and encouraging me to keep at it. I hope I don't omit the name of anyone who deserves my thanks, but I ask forgiveness in advance of any omissions, just in case. My promise (to myself) is that, next book, I'll maintain an ongoing list for the acknowledgments while I'm writing! Here goes:

Starting with my immediate family, my four grandchildren are able and enthusiastic readers but still too young to help me write a book with anything more than their love, hugs, and laughter, but believe me, I cherish each one. The generation of their parents, my "kids," is a consistent source of valuable information as well as support. Debby Ziff Cook is one of the best editors I know, and I trust her to smooth and clarify any early draft I've written; this book was no exception. Jamie Cook, her husband, serves as my unofficial art and/or legal advisor if and as needed. Amy Ziff and her husband, Jeff Glueck, are usually my first stop for the "how to" of marketing strategies and for guidance through the technical morass of our world. (Even though Jeff always reminds me that I'm the most tech savvy of all the grandparents in our clan, there's a lot of guesswork that would be exercised on my part without their help.)

More thanks than words alone can convey go to Lynne Dodson, my friend and colleague of many years, going back to our days at Bridgeport Hospital, an "11 yellow" if there ever was one. She is indeed the perfect counterpoint to my "12 red." Not for the first time, Lynne has earned my everlasting appreciation and respect. I cannot picture making this book happen without her.

A special thank-you to my accomplished, talented, and thoughtful cardiologist, Suzanne Steinbaum, who believed in the importance of this book from our first discussion of it, and who graciously guided me to Sarah Jane Freymann, literary agent, whose wisdom, tenacity, and determination brought the proposal to my enthusiastic acquisitions editor, Suzanne Staszak-Silva, and to its publishing home at Rowman & Littlefield. I am forever appreciative of this circle of women and their tireless good energies.

Since 2006, I've been fortunate to be part of Thursday-morning "facconfs" at Mt. Sinai Medical Center, led by Hillel Swiller, MD, director of the Division of Psychotherapy in the Department of Psychiatry. Hillel; Phil Luloff, MD; Jeff Golland, PhD; and the large group (nearly 50 percent of whom are women!) have been enthusiastic supporters of my project. It was, in fact, a presentation I made at this conference, and the group's significant, positive response to it, that sealed my determination to make my story into a book and "get it out there" to as many people as possible. My goal: to describe and teach the value of conversations about end-of-life matters, whether wishes or data, or both. The group is too large to thank everyone by name, but you each know who you are, and I hope you realize how much your interest, support, and friendships mean to me.

Turning to readers of my early drafts, friends and colleagues who offered informal edits, discussed titles, volunteered stories, and were cheerleaders throughout, my appreciation is of your patience as well as of your good ideas and friendship. This group includes Elena Lesser Bruun, EdD; Nils Bruun; Judy Cohen; Karen Davis, PhD; Walt Ehrhardt, EdD; Judith Felsenfeld; Michael Glueck, MD; Mimi Glueck; Seth Koch, DVM; Trudi Levine; my maternal cousin Henry Lowenstein, PhD; Eileen Lubars; Judith Marks-White; Linda Marshall; Paul Miller, DC; David Earl Platts, PhD; Pearl Sheps; Sheldon Sheps, MD; John Stine; and Shira Zaguri. Barbara Selman Jay never turns away my late-night telephone calls (not even when we were in seventh grade together)! Mitch Anthony, with whom I share experiences of living in Rochester, Minnesota, was generous with both his time and suggestions for my project. Bill Shapiro, Ken Schwartz, and Carmine Zut, cochairs of the Issues of Aging Special Interest Group at American Group Psychotherapy Association (AGPA), have been consistent supporters of this project. My thanks also to Lee Kassan, editor of the Eastern Group Psychotherapy Society's journal.

An important shout-out to an old friend and very talented colleague, Mauro Marinelli, who has not yet seen the book but whose own two volumes, of both photographs and written words, have been an inspiration to me. When you believe in a project, giving up is not an option.

Tobias Moss and Sarah Krinsky, Rabbinic Fellows at Congregation B'nai Jeshurun NYC, were responsive and helpful, speedily answering my last-minute questions, and I thank them enormously. I'm a member of the B'nai Jeshurun committee, Aging in Place, chaired by a trio including Rochelle Friedlich, and I've discussed the book's topic there. Lizzie Kraiem has been generous with her knowledge of Ethical Wills, and I'm so glad we made time to talk together.

Last, but certainly not least important, I want to thank each person who has been in my practice and participated in my workshops or lectures over these five years. Most of you have been aware of the time I've spent researching, preparing, and writing this book, and were interested in its progress. In some cases, elements of your experiences, as well as those of my family, colleagues, and friends, have been woven into stories in the text. While I've protected identities in every case, you will, I suspect, experience a glimmer of recognition, and perhaps even a smile, when you read some modified version of your own experiences.

Index

accident, 49–50
accomplishments: bucket list in relation to, 30; with competition, 100, 102–3; reflection on, 100–101, 102
accuracy, 23
achievements. *See* accomplishments
acknowledgment: of communication heritage, 26; of death, xiii–xiv, 127; of feelings, 79; of life experiences, 137; of wishes by Listeners, 9, 66
adventure, 10–11
affection: as Listener quality, 36; regret in relation to, 104
aging: denial of, 127; humor for healthy, 17–19; as taboo topic, 12–13
Americans, 73–74
anniversary, 65, 71
anxiety, xii; for attorney regarding redistribution of assets, 112–14; exercises for, 79; greeting in relation to, 78–79; silence causing, 109
art, graphic, 97
assessment: exercises for Listener, 40; of family issues, 57–58
assets: attorney anxiety regarding redistribution of, 112–14; identification of primary, 53;

obstacles with distribution of, 116–17
attorney: anxiety regarding redistribution of assets, 112–14; for Last Will and Testament, 45, 48; Listener informed on power of, 52, 69
audio recordings, 23
audiovisuals, 97
avoidance: of conversation, 15, 127; of sarcasm, 128

beauty, 119, 122
birthday, 29–30
book group: consideration for, xii–xiii; guide for, 139–48
book project: conversation, 108–10; personal experience for, 33–34; reflection on, 127–28, 129; reflection recommendation, 119
bucket list: desensitization, 13; exercises, 29–30; experiment, 31; as precursor, 28

calmness, 4
Can't We Talk About Something More Pleasant? (Chast), 26
capability, 36

About the Author

Anne Finkelman Ziff is a licensed marriage and family therapist in private practice in New York City and assistant clinical professor, Department of Psychiatry, Icahn School of Medicine at Mt. Sinai Medical Center, New York. Prior to her licensure as a therapist, Ziff was a corporate writer at Pitney Bowes and Bridgeport Hospital and a journalist. She spent five dynamic years as Arts & Entertainment editor of *The Fairfield Citizen News* and at the *Westport News*, both in Fairfield County, Connecticut, where she was actively involved, writing a weekly column, "All the World's a Stage . . ." and reviewing the many cultural activities and personalities in the greater Westport community. Previous professional books include *Marrying Well: The Clinician's Guide to Premarital Therapy* that includes a provocative, original paradigm: *The Eight Premarital Stages*. Ziff lectures and conducts workshops in addition to her private practice and work at Mt. Sinai. Her website is afztalk2me.com.